THE REVOLU

IONARY WAR

AMERICA'S FIGHT FOR FREEDOM

By Bart McDowell
NATIONAL GEOGRAPHIC, *Senior Editorial Staff*

Prepared by Special Publications Division,
Robert L. Breeden, *Chief*

NATIONAL GEOGRAPHIC SOCIETY, WASHINGTON, D. C.
Melvin M. Payne, *President*
Melville Bell Grosvenor, *Editor-in-Chief*
Gilbert M. Grosvenor, *Editor*

The Revolutionary War
by Bart McDowell
National Geographic Senior Editorial Staff

Published by The National Geographic Society

Melvin M. Payne, *President*
Melville Bell Grosvenor, *Editor-in-Chief*
Gilbert M. Grosvenor, *Editor*

Dr. John R. Alden, *Consultant*
James B. Duke Professor of History in Duke University

Prepared by The Special Publications Division

Robert L. Breeden, *Editor*
Donald J. Crump, *Associate Editor*
Mary Ann Harrell, *Research and Style*
Tee Loftin Snell, Peggy Winston, *Research*
Betty Strauss Kosco, *Illustrations Research*
Ronald M. Fisher, Mary Ann Harrell,
    Geraldine Linder, Gerald S. Snyder, *Picture Legends*
Luba Balko, Margaret S. Dean, *Editorial Assistants*

Illustrations and Design
Donald J. Crump, *Picture Editor*
Geraldine Linder, *Assistant Picture Editor*
Joseph A. Taney, *Art Director*
Josephine B. Bolt, *Designer*

Production and Printing
Ronald M. Fisher, Robert W. Messer, *Production*
James R. Whitney, *Engraving and Printing*
John R. Metcalfe, *Assistant, Engraving and Printing*

Richard Schlecht, *Paintings pages 62-63,
    104-105, 118-119, 166-167; Maps pages 26, 38-39,
    57, 68, 89, 103, 117, 142, 188-189*
Virginia L. Baza, John D. Garst, Jr., Ann Ruhnka,
    Leo B. Zebarth, *Map Research and Production*
Dorothy Corson, Jolene McCoy, *Index*

Third printing 1972
Standard Book Number 87044-047-0
Library of Congress Catalog Card Number 67-25820

Author Bart McDowell steadies George Washington's own spyglass for his 4-year-old son Rob at Mount Vernon, Washington's home in northern Virginia. Mrs. McDowell, daughter Tina, age 12, and Josh, 10, wait their turns as 15-year-old Kel props the telescope on his head. Visits here kindled an interest in 18th-century history that inspired the McDowells to retrace the footsteps of those patriots who fought and won the Revolutionary War.

NATIONAL GEOGRAPHIC PHOTOGRAPHER WINFIELD PARKS

OVERLEAF—RIDING INTO THE MIDST OF A BRITISH BAYONET ATTACK, GENERAL WASHINGTON
RALLIES HIS MEN TO VICTORY AT THE BATTLE OF PRINCETON (PAINTING BY JOHN TRUMBULL,
YALE UNIVERSITY ART GALLERY). PAGE 1—BRONZE MEDALLION FROM A DOOR TO THE SENATE
WING OF THE U. S. CAPITOL: A NEW JERSEY FARMER STRUGGLES WITH A HESSIAN MERCENARY.

Foreword

CANDLES threw a gold, quivering light around the rebuilt House of Burgesses as we took our seats. My wife and I were revisiting Williamsburg, Virginia, and we had brought a friend from Ceylon to show her this favorite vignette of America's colonial past. But now, everything seemed so different, so much more alive.

I had just read Bart McDowell's fascinating manuscript and reviewed the splendid illustrations for this book. The 18th century had absorbed me. For the first time I was truly conscious of the individuals who had made history here: young, freckle-faced Tom Jefferson, the untidily dressed Patrick Henry, and that towering tight-lipped planter George Washington.

The essence of this book is personal involvement. As readers, we travel in the shadow of people who waged the Revolutionary War. We overhear their gossip, read newspapers over their shoulders, even browse through their letters. We look at the sketches and paintings that their artists made; we see color photographs of their homes, their money, their weapons, their maps. Soon their viewpoints—and even their ideals—become more meaningful.

Everyone will find his own favorite character in this book, for here are people in all the variety of life itself. Paul Revere is not just a distant, galloping horseman; he tells his adventure story for himself. Here is that good and grizzled warrior Dan Morgan with his battle scars still visible. And here Rebecca Motte offers to burn down her own home to drive out the redcoats—then generously invites her British prisoners back to dinner!

Throughout our book we rediscover life in the 1770's and '80's. The McDowell family travels to the battlefields and historic sites to visit not just places, but also times and seasons. On horseback they ride Paul Revere's famous route, and shiver in Christmas snow at Trenton just as Washington did. Readers will share this personal adventure and perhaps even find a new family hobby. For this book was planned for the home library, and the illustrated format will appeal to readers of any age.

I believe every American family should be steeped in the traditions of our founding fathers and should know, too, how those traditions took shape from the very face of our country. For our land—its mountains, rivers, and valleys—deeply influenced the lives of the patriots, as it has our nation's growth. But I am far from the first to voice this belief.

Soon after our Declaration of Independence, John Adams wrote his wife, "America is our Country, and . . . Knowledge of its Geography, is most important to Us and our Children." Adams then promised to send a list of all available maps: "You will ask me why I trouble you with all these. . . . I answer, that I may turn the Attention of the Family to the subject of American Geography."

So be it done, Mr. Adams.

Gilbert M. Grosvenor

Redcoats sack a New England home before the eyes of a helpless family. Such acts throughout the war

Contents

PAINTING BY ALFRED WORDSWORTH THOMPSON, CONNECTICUT HISTORICAL SOCIETY

embittered patriots and caused them to renounce irrevocably their allegiance to the British Crown.

Raising a liberty pole, cheering colonists demonstrate their opposition to tyranny and their devotion to

1774: "The Rebellious Disposition"

freedom. After July 4, 1776, liberty poles stood for a new union of thirteen embattled American states.

A MIZZLING APRIL MIST had dampened the three-cornered hats, the muskets, and the Minutemen. Now a stern voice ordered retreat.

"No battle today!" the voice called out. "Our powder is getting wet. We will have no re-enactment of the Battle of Concord."

But a moment later—in an interval just long enough for curiosity to twitch at a trigger—I heard a shot: close, loud, anonymous. With a father's reflexes, I grabbed for the hands of my two nearest children.

"The battle must be on again!" someone shouted in the roiling crowd. Many Minutemen had come to the same conclusion, and plainly not all of the powder was wet. Muskets thundered all around, flashing red flame and spewing sulphuric smoke. I steered the children from the bridge toward a safe grassy slope. The scent of gunpowder clung to us, and our ears were ringing.

"I thought they had called off the battle," said my daughter Tina. And then she asked

9

the same simple question that is forever the goad of historians: "How did it all start?"

All of us wondered the same thing. The six of us—my wife Martha and our four children—had come to Massachusetts as proper sightseers to watch an orderly pageant recalling the first battle of the American Revolution. Instead we had ourselves taken part in a spontaneous jumble of men and guns.

"How did it all start?" Tina had asked.

"Accidentally," I conceded. "And also because everything was ready for it. Just like the real Revolutionary War."

Our interest in the American Revolution had also started accidentally. We live in Virginia's Fairfax County. These are the same green hills hunted and tilled by our late neighbor George Washington and admired by each of his Presidential heirs. History hems us in: The Potomac defines one county line and Bull Run another. Often we take a houseguest to see Mount Vernon; on weekends we visit Williamsburg and Philadelphia.

Our oldest son Kel studied American history in seventh grade with a gifted teacher who, as it happened, is a British subject. The class turned into a year-long, zestful, successful rebellion. While preparing rebuttals for his teacher, Kel even found a history hero: the artillery general, Henry Knox.

"Think of it," said he. "Knox was only a fat bookseller—and he learned everything about guns from his own books!"

We, too, relied on books, but not entirely. Tina, our horse-happy daughter, at first found the Revolution exciting because of the transportation. From Paul Revere's ride to the exploits of Light-Horse Harry Lee, Tina rarely heard the cannon over the jangle of spurs. Josh, two years younger than his sister and quite the soldiering boy, arranged battles with model Minutemen and lead redcoats.

The youngest of us was our toddler and only illiterate, Robert. At first he was a burden to us all, but as he gradually became a happy traveler, he joined in our family hobby

and understood far more than we expected.

On holidays we traveled to Revolutionary War sites. We could not, of course, take each battle in its chronological sequence, starting with Lexington and ending with Yorktown. But we did try to see each site at its own most appropriate season. We visited Philadelphia and Independence Hall on the Fourth of July; and—although Valley Forge was only 20 miles farther—made a special trip to see it in the chill of winter.

At first, we were interested mostly in the atmosphere, but soon we saw the importance

At Williamsburg, capital of Virginia till 1780, royal governors found a "Palace" worthy of the Empire, and colonists ready to stand up for their rights. From year to year, in 13 colonies, policies made in London provoked discussion and dissent among Americans. And militia companies rehearsed the manual of arms, as citizens of Williamsburg perform it today on Market Square.

NATIONAL GEOGRAPHIC PHOTOGRAPHERS B. ANTHONY STEWART (BELOW) AND JAMES L. STANFIELD

"I rely on the hearts of my subjects, the only true support of the Crown," declared George III. Yet by his rigid views of royal duty he forfeited affection within his Empire and his own family. In 1771 Their Majesties George and Charlotte boasted six children (of an eventual 15); at left, in rose satin, stands the future George IV, who grew up to loathe his inflexible father. On official buildings in the colonies the Royal Arms evoked pride and loyalty — but revenue stamps of 1765, with the same device, stirred Americans to furious protests against taxation by Act of Parliament.

of season in the war itself. Monmouth was a battle fought in a blazing heat wave — hence the heroism of Molly Pitcher taking water to thirsty men. We visited the icy Delaware River and the scene of Washington's historic crossing as twilight died on snowdrifts; and only then could we understand the sacrifice patriots made to surprise the Hessians in Trenton. Thus we moved from the warm ooze of mossy Carolina swamps to the breathless, brittle cold of wintertime Quebec.

Scholars were our scouts. We collected

solid books along with tricornes, firelocks, and postcards. Our family bulletin board on the kitchen wall grew heavy with War bulletins: pictures of Revolutionary uniforms, facsimiles of recruiting posters and contemporary newspapers.

"That bulletin board is our time machine!" said Josh. He had a point, for breakfast conversation often shifted to the gossip of history. Robert was about three years old, I guess, the day he examined the portrait on a one-dollar bill.

"George Washington," he said solemnly. "He's dead, isn't he?" Then he added with stubborn loyalty, "But he's still our friend!"

ON EVERYDAY DRIVES to work or school or market, we cross Braddock Road. A traveler could follow it—and its tributaries—all the way to Pittsburgh. This was the route taken by the scarlet-coated Maj. Gen. Edward Braddock on his springtime journey in 1755. The dogwood was blooming when he left his headquarters in Fairfax County and marched

13

smartly northward toward disaster and death.

"Was General Braddock on our side?" Josh asked. I explained that Braddock fought in the French and Indian War 20 years before our rebellion against Britain. "Then why didn't we teach him to fight Indian style?"

The frontier French and their allied Indians, of course, did all the teaching. On July 9, 1755, on the forested banks of the Monongahela, they cut down the proud Britons and shot General Braddock through the lungs. He lingered for days, pondering his mistakes, then found breath to say, "We shall better know how to deal with them another time."

But time he did not have. When Braddock died, his aide, a young Virginian, buried the general in a road so that wagon tracks could hide the grave from victorious savages. Braddock's only monument was a dark memory that haunted a whole generation of soldiers.

What was it like, that terrifying ambush? Years later, the same Virginia aide told how he rode his horse through the battlefield at night among "shocking scenes...the dead, the dying, the groans, lamentations and cries along the road of the wounded for help...."

Those strangely moving words belong to a man never famous for eloquence or emotion. But George Washington was just 23 when he joined Braddock's staff; this was his first big battle. His later military service anointed him with glory and even with office,

OCTOBER 31, 1765; HISTORICAL
SOCIETY OF PENNSYLVANIA

Ominous parody announces the "expiring" issue of the Pennsylvania Journal. *It stopped publication to avoid buying the expensive stamps required by law for each edition.*

"If this be treason, make the most of it!" Patrick Henry of Virginia flings down the gauntlet of defiance to the Stamp Act and the king who signed it. Fellow legislators cry out in horror. He had hinted that George III might die as a murdered tyrant. Peter Rothermel painted the Burgesses' chamber long after fire destroyed the Capitol; and 40 years after Henry gave his daring speech, a biographer set it down from old men's memories.

RED HILL SHRINE, BROOKNEAL, VIRGINIA

for he was elected in 1758 to the House of Burgesses, lower house of Virginia's legislature. Few of his comrades were so lucky.

From our perspective of two centuries, we can examine this moment of history, the men who made it, and the way their lives would braid with future events. Benjamin Franklin, for example, collected Pennsylvania wagons to carry Braddock's provisions.

"Maybe Franklin found the very wagon that Daniel Morgan drove!" suggested Josh. My second son was especially proud of the wagoner Morgan, our grizzled neighbor from Winchester, Virginia. Later, when Josh found that Morgan became a general, he took a personal pride in the wagoner's achievement.

In the same spirit—like the chorus in a Greek drama—we ticked off a list of other officers from the colonial conflict we call the French and Indian War. Typical of the personalities were two future generals who were wounded in Braddock's campaign. Now Thomas Gage and Horatio Gates had come to a fork in their fates. Gates would make his home in Virginia and cast his lot with America. Gage would remain in the service of the king and grow so greatly in rank and caution as to win a palace nickname, "the mild general."

In Europe, where this struggle was called the Seven Years' War, a generation was trained and tested in battle. A German captain named von Steuben won a letter of thanks from Frederick the Great of Prussia, fighting with Britain against France and allied powers. But after the Battle of Minden a court martial of Britons found one lieutenant general "unfit to serve His Majesty in any military capacity whatsoever." The same man, as Lord George Germain, would become the wartime Secretary of State for the Colonies.

And what was this war's legacy for the very young? With the hindsight of history, we consult biographies today and see a French lad orphaned by the Battle of Minden and far too young for grief. Years will pass before the boy Marquis de Lafayette vows vengeance upon the British. But now we check another book and find a certain swarthy, pale-eyed youth who has deserted his military post on the American frontier. Is this just a juvenile muddle—or is it perhaps a portent? Our chorus knows and pities this youngster, for we read his name: Benedict Arnold.

In its far-flung struggle, Great Britain, led

by William Pitt, finally won the war. The Treaty of Paris of 1763 settled the terms but not the problems of peace. The Bourbon king of France was humiliated; he gave the region beyond the Mississippi to Spain. Except for a few rocky islands, all of French North America was gone—all Canada went to Britain.

Great Britain's new king, the young, high-minded George III, now reigned over the mightiest empire in the world. True, his treasury had a larger national debt than any in its records: £130,000,000. But surely the American colonies could help pay for their own defense. Politicians considered methods: perhaps a sale of stamps? Or duties on imported goods? Meantime, there were leftover war supplies to tend, like those cannon out at Fort Ticonderoga on the New York frontier. Thus the debits and credits from one war would affect the fortunes of another.

WHEN I WAS A BOY studying American history, George III was presented as a black-hearted tyrant. The picture was false. "He was one of the most conscientious sovereigns who ever sat upon the English throne," wrote that great honorary American Sir Winston Churchill. "Simple in his tastes.... He possessed great moral courage...."

When I read these words to my youngsters, they remained skeptical; after all, Sir Winston was British. And so I showed my young doubters a commentary on King George's character that we called a report card. It comes to us from Lord Waldegrave, George's tutor-governor for four years, who penned it when his pupil had just turned 20.

Patrick Henry's words enthrall the author, his family, and other visitors as a Williamsburg guide recites them in the Hall of the House of Burgesses, heart of the rebuilt Capitol. Eyewitness notes on the speech came to light in 1921. A French agent had heard "henery" ask pardon for his boldness and profess perfect loyalty to the king as well as to "his Countrys Dying liberty." Yet Henry inspired the House to pass "resolves" against the Stamp Act; his own draft of them lies under glass on the clerk's table today. Newspapers throughout the colonies roused the public by reprinting them in full. At left, Josh and Tina McDowell watch a journeyman "beater" ink his type just as printers did in 1765.

"He is strictly honest," it said, "but wants that frank and open behavior which makes honesty appear amiable.... His religion is free from all hypocrisy, but is not ... charitable.... He has ... too much obstinacy.... He ... will seldom do wrong, except when he mistakes wrong for right...."

Tina read that report card, stumbled at a word or two, and asked, "Did George pass or fail?" At least we know that two years later, on the death of his grandfather, he was promoted from Prince of Wales to King.

Scrupulous and devout, George III called his era "the wickedest age that ever was seen." He greatly feared any faction that would "reduce the Sovereign to a mere tool in its hands." He insisted that "the Executive power" must remain "where the Constitution has placed it" —with the king. From his ministers he demanded a loyal obedience.

By 1764 English landowners were insisting that taxes come down to peacetime levels. To make up the difference in revenue, the king's minister George Grenville — "Gentle Shepherd," Pitt called him — looked for other sheep in far pastures. He began to enforce laws that had long gathered dust in the New World. Customs officers were ordered into action. Colonial governors were told to aid them. The Royal Navy began hunting

17

Engrav'd Printed & Sold by Paul Revere Boston

smugglers along the North American coast.

A new Sugar Act, with an enforceable duty on West Indies molasses, sharply hurt New England rum-makers. Even worse, colonial merchants had always earned hard cash by trading with the sugar-producing islands of the Spanish and French West Indies; now they would lack gold or silver to buy their English goods. On top of these troubles, a Currency Act banned paper money as legal tender and aggravated a depression that had paralyzed business in the colonies.

Thus Gentle Shepherd Grenville could shear few sheep. His import duties did not bring in large sums, so he proposed a new tax on the colonies: the Stamp Act of 1765.

Stamps, of course, were familiar folderol in England, adorning all kinds of documents as receipts for tax paid and earning some £300,000 a year. But stamps were unfamiliar in the New World—and never before had Parliament taxed the colonies for revenue.

A friend of America, Col. Isaac Barré, warned Parliament in vain that the colonists would resist, as good "sons of liberty." He had judged them shrewdly.

The Stamp Act offended just about everybody. One article levied a £2 tax on each university or college degree in the colonies. Similarly, colonial lawyers were required to use stamps on almost all their documents. But as if it were not enough to anger scholars and lawyers, the Stamp Act also proposed taxes for newspapers and taverns. At once

Boston's "Bloody Massacre" of March 5, 1770, lives in folklore as Paul Revere engraved it: wanton slaughter of respectable citizens by soldiers of a tyrant. Eyewitnesses on oath told a different story: a hardbitten, hostile mob taunting frightened troops until they answered insults and clubs with their muskets in self-defense. Juries in Boston acquitted the soldiers of murder. But throughout New England Revere's prints and Sam Adams's pamphlets fostered fear and distrust of Britain. Now the "massacre" victims lie near Revere, Adams, and other heroes of the Revolution in the Old Granary Burying Ground, in the shadow of Park Street Congregational Church—and their graves have become a quiet shrine.

angry pamphlets and handbills began to flutter through North America, and the taverns echoed with oaths aimed at tyranny.

Benjamin Franklin, now 59 years old, was serving the colonies as a spokesman and lobbyist in London. He had opposed the Stamp Act, but, as he wrote to a friend, "We might as well have hinder'd the Suns setting."

Franklin's daughter Sarah reported the excitement in America: "The Subject now is the Stamp Act and nothing else is talked of; the Dutch talk of the Stomp ack, the Negroes of the tamp; in short every body has something to say."

The varied accents of Pennsylvania were now joined by a golden voice from frontier Virginia. A scruffily dressed young man named Patrick Henry planned his debut on May 29—his own 29th birthday. The date provided still another irony, for this was the anniversary Parliament itself had set aside for "Thanksgiving...for...the Restitution of the King...in the Year 1660." An 18th-century *Book of Common Prayer* that I bought years ago spells out the liturgy on its frail, rag-paper pages: the vow of "all loyal and dutiful allegiance to thine Anointed Servant," the Epistle ("Fear God. Honour the King."), and the Gospel ("Render therefore unto Cesar the things which are Cesar's...").

Henry prepared some similar phrases on King and Caesar. First he introduced some radical resolutions. Then he breathed his brimstone. The audience fell silent, shocked by the words that carefully skirted sedition.

Seated in the elegant, reconstructed Hall of the House of Burgesses in Williamsburg, we could almost hear the echo of a legendary warning: "Caesar had his Brutus; Charles the First, his Cromwell; and George the Third— *may profit by their example.*"

"Nice!" whispered Tina as she slipped onto the dark bench. "But I thought the room would be bigger." So do others accustomed to the size of the Capitol in Washington. Yet Patrick Henry's oratory won a favorable vote; his colleagues accepted four of his "resolves." We saw his own copy displayed under glass on a table in the House of Burgesses:

"Resolved That the first Adventurers and Settlers of this his Majesties Colony and Dominion brought with them and transmitted to their Posterity . . . all the Privileges . . . held . . . by the People of Great Britain."

The paper may turn golden and the ink go brown, but the words make a lasting point. When I asked Kel what he thought of them, he fingered the green felt on the table top for a moment.

"They still thought of themselves as Englishmen," he said, quite rightly. These men were not begging for new liberties or for independent nationhood. Instead, they feared the loss of freedoms they had already long enjoyed. Elected bodies like this one in Virginia had always levied local taxes; some voted the salaries of governors and clerks. As good Englishmen, these men well knew that power follows purse strings.

So the Burgesses voted the Virginia Resolves, the first official answer to the Stamp Act. At that instant, Patrick Henry, age 29, became a radical leader in Virginia.

In Boston, another career was suddenly advanced by hatred of the Stamp Act. Until now Samuel Adams had spent most of his 43 years in a chaos of paper and books. His family and his Harvard education were good, but he spent his time on town politics and ran

Rhode Island smugglers board and burn the revenue cutter Gaspée, *aground near Providence on June 9, 1772. They overpowered the crew and wounded the captain, who had tried to enforce the customs laws. In fact, prominent merchants led this affair without any disguise at all. No one would name them to a Crown commission of inquiry, even for rewards of £500.*

through his modest inheritance. Then voters elected him town scavenger and later tax collector. His cousin John Adams appraised Sam Adams as a "universal good character" but "too attentive to the public, and not enough to himself and his family."

Now Sam Adams became even more attentive to mobs. In August, the streets of Boston went wild. The newly named stamp officer was besieged in his own home and so frightened that he resigned. The tumult grew. And in September, Samuel Adams was elected to the Massachusetts legislature. Meanwhile couriers on post roads were keeping local groups called Sons of Liberty in careful concert.

Moderate leaders were still in control when the Massachusetts legislature called the convention known as the Stamp Act Congress. Nine colonies sent 27 delegates to New York in October to consider "a general and united, dutiful, loyal and humble Representation of their Condition to His Majesty and the Parliament...."

Throughout the colonies, men planned demonstrations for November 1, the day when the Stamp Act took effect. Shops closed. Ships ran down their colors to half mast. Bells tolled. At Portsmouth, a coffin was paraded through the streets; it bore the word *Liberty*. From New England to Georgia citizens boycotted the stamps.

Parliament listened thoughtfully to the merchants in their own midst; the American colonies, after all, were the best market in the Empire. So the Stamp Act was repealed in early 1766.

Our revolution might have ended there, if Parliament had stopped. But Parliament did not stop. The brilliant and irresponsible Charles Townshend, "Champagne Charlie," took over Grenville's role. In lightheaded style he ignored the fate of the stamp tax. Parliament passed his notorious Townshend Acts in 1767, reorganizing the customs service and laying new duties on such everyday items as glass, lead, paint, paper, and tea.

Astonished and indignant Americans began to suspect the king's ministers of conspiring against colonial rights. Many objected as strongly as the young printer Isaiah Thomas, whose *Massachusetts Spy* denounced the customs regime as "a Troop of Cossacks."

Samuel Adams, "father of the Revolution," points to the Massachusetts Charter, symbol of his colony's rights. Nobody could doubt—or prove—his responsibility for the Boston Tea Party of December 16, 1773. That night townsmen dressed as Mohawks in war paint tossed 342 chests of fine but taxable tea into the harbor. Next morning, says tradition, this rare chest with Chinese lacquer work washed ashore. Soon Parliament, insulted beyond endurance, passed the "Intolerable Acts" to subdue the Bay Colony. But these laws created unity for resistance and rebellion.

SKETCH BY A. LASSELL RIPLEY, THE PAUL REVERE LIFE INSURANCE COMPANY, WORCESTER, MASSACHUSETTS

Penelope Barker presided, as North Carolinians recall, when 51 ladies met at Edenton on October 25, 1774, to renounce British tea in the name of liberty. Now a bronze teapot marks the site of their party, the home of Mistress Elizabeth King. The Barker house, built about 1782 and moved for restoration in 1952, stands framed by cannon. The story goes that patriots saved these guns in 1778 when the French ship that brought them ran aground in shallow Albemarle Sound.

CUPOLA HOUSE LIBRARY AND MUSEUM, INCORPORATED

And so in fact they seemed to shipowner John Hancock, heir to an uncle's mercantile fortune. A popular fellow with jut-jawed good looks, Hancock was Boston's richest man and, through his friendship with Sam Adams, the chief financier for radical colonial propaganda.

On May 9, 1768, Hancock's sloop *Liberty* sailed into harbor from the Portuguese isles of Madeira. For years the colonies had imported Madeira wines without trouble; and they had paid the Portuguese with barrel staves manufactured in New England. The newly enforced laws, involving a very high duty, would have hurt the wine merchants, the stave-makers, and the shipowners—had

anyone taken them very seriously. The skipper of Hancock's sloop *Liberty* did not.

The murk of argument still hides what really happened. Probably, a minor customs official named Thomas Kirk boarded the sloop that first night in port—but Kirk was seized and locked below decks for three hours; during that time, he heard "a Noise as of many people upon deck at Work hoisting out Goods"—smuggled wine, presumably.

Abruptly Boston customs men seized the *Liberty* at Hancock's wharf and put Royal Marines aboard. A waterfront crowd watched in amazement and then in anger. The marines towed the *Liberty* out into the harbor, and moored her beside the gunboat *Romney.* Now the crowd turned into a mob, rampaging through Boston's cobbled streets, roughing up the officials, and finally dragging a customs officer's barge to Boston Common and setting fire to it.

The colony's attorney general brought charges against Hancock for "landing ... one hundred Pipes of Wine ... with Intent to defraud the said Lord the King."

Defending Hancock was an able young lawyer named John Adams. Like his fiery cousin Sam, John Adams had a facile pen. But unlike Sam, John was a man of tidy habits, devoted to the study and practice of law which, he felt, "does not dissolve the Obligations of Morality or of Religion."

The *Liberty* case dragged on for months — "a painful Drudgery" John Adams called it. "I was thoroughly weary and disgusted with

the Court, ... the Cause, and even with the tyrannical Bell that dongled me out of my House every Morning."

The very duration of the case, before the Crown dropped the charges, kept the issue bubbling. So did the ship's name, for who could miss the symbolism of *Liberty* seized?

Tempers rose. British troops arrived in Boston, and Sam Adams encouraged townsmen to taunt "the lobster backs," as hotheads called them. And then on a nasty evening in March, 1770, a gang of noisy young men began to badger the British sentry at the east end of the Old State House. The youths tossed some snowballs. Clubs flew. Then shouts. From the guard post across the street, more British troops hurried over the ice-slickened cobbles. The mob was growing, its disposition as raw as the weather. Shouts dared the soldiers to fire their muskets. Finally, a few took the dare.

After the shots — and the cries in the darkness and the confusion of shadows — the whole bitter crowd drew in its breath. Some of the townsmen lay crumpled in the snow.

James
Bay

HUDSON'S BAY COMPANY

Lake Superior

Saguenay

St. Lawrence

C A N A D A *Ottawa*

QUEBEC ✕

Chaudière R.

MONTREAL • *Richelieu R.*

MAINE
(a part of Mass.)

Lake
Champlain

FORT
TICONDEROGA ▫

Connecticut

▫ FORT
WESTERN

Lake Huron

Lake Ontario

ORISKANY ✕

SARATOGA ✕

N.H.

ALBANY •

NEWBURYPORT •

FORT DETROIT ▫

Lake Erie

Allegheny

NEW YORK

MASS.

BOSTON •

WEST POINT ▫

Hudson

CONN. R.I.

Illinois

Wabash

WYOMING MASSACRE ✕

MORRISTOWN •
• NEW YORK

QUEBEC
BOUNDARY BY ACT OF 1774

PITTSBURGH •

PENNSYLVANIA

Susquehanna R.

Monongahela

TRENTON •

Delaware R.

✕ MONMOUTH
COURTHOUSE

Missouri

VALLEY FORGE ▫
PHILADELPHIA •

N.J.

VINCENNES ▫
(FORT SACKVILLE)

Ohio

Potomac

MD.

• HEAD OF ELK

▫ KASKASKIA

ALEXANDRIA •
MOUNT VERNON •

ANNAPOLIS •

DEL.

Atlantic Ocean

VIRGINIA

James

*Chesapeake
Bay*

BOUNDARY BY
PROCLAMATION, 1763

RICHMOND •

WILLIAMSBURG • ✕ YORKTOWN

• NORFOLK

ELIZABETHTON

Tennessee

✕ GUILFORD
COURTHOUSE

• EDENTON

Mississippi

INDIAN RESERVE
BY PROCLAMATION, 1763

NORTH CAROLINA

• CHARLOTTE

COWPENS ✕
THE WAXHAWS ✕
HOBKIRK'S HILL ✕
NINETY SIX ✕ CAMDEN ✕

✕ KINGS MOUNTAIN

✕ MOORES CREEK

KETTLE CREEK ✕
AUGUSTA •

SOUTH CAROLINA

▫ FORT MOTTE
• FORT WATSON
✕ EUTAW SPRINGS
• CHARLESTON

Tombigbee

Savannah

GEORGIA

Chattahoochee

BOUNDARY BY ROYAL ORDER, 1764

• SAVANNAH

▫ FORT SUNBURY

BOUNDARY BY PROCLAMATION, 1763

WEST FLORIDA

• ST. AUGUSTINE

Gulf of Mexico

EAST
FLORIDA

His Majesty's most
prized colonies become a battle-
ground: Boundaries drawn in
prewar years cannot contain the
forces unleashed in 1775. On the eve
of revolution, the 13 rebellious prov-
inces held about 2,500,000 people,
checked from westward expansion
into lands reserved for Indians, including
the Ohio country marked off as part of Quebec
in 1774. In London, two months' voyage
away, the king and his ministers confidently made plans and policies for a
continent that not a man among
them had ever seen. Through years of
fighting, they would learn to recognize
place-names in America—flourishing
coastal cities or tiny inland hamlets
—by news of British victories and defeats.

✕ BATTLES   ▫ FORTS

0   300
STATUTE MILES

Touring his country's post roads, Benjamin Franklin stops his chaise for a mug of fresh milk at a wayside house. As deputy postmaster-general for British North America, he traveled hundreds of bumpy miles in 1754 and again in 1763 to improve the speed of the mails. His efficient postal system drew the colonies together. When tensions rose in the 1770's, patriot couriers rode his routes with secret dispatches for revolutionary committees of correspondence in the provincial towns.

The places where they fell are still marked by plaques on the street, for this was the Boston Massacre. Like countless other visitors my family viewed the scene from the vantage of the Old State House; we even climbed out on the balcony and leaned warily over the rail to watch the city traffic move across and buff the bronze markers. Standing there, I marveled that only five men died, for there was hatred enough for a hundred, and enemies were crowded close in these narrow streets. Of all the participants here, I most admired Thomas Hutchinson.

"Who in the world was that?" asked Josh.

"The lieutenant governor then," I told him. "He was a scholar, more at home with history

books than with armies." But that night he came out into the midst of the furious crowd. He risked assassination — but he talked the mob and soldiers into going home.

Hutchinson promised the Bostonians a fair trial for the soldiers who had fired on the crowd. And he kept his promise. The Crown did not want to hang His Majesty's soldiers. Nor did the attorneys defending them want to prove that Bostonians were to blame. John Adams, in fact, proved that he loved justice more than popularity; he defended the British soldiers against the charge of murder, and they went free.

Meantime, Parliament reconsidered the Townshend Acts, and dropped all the hated duties — except for the one on tea. Prosperity rapidly returned to America. In London Lord North, the obedient Prime Minister of King George III, seemed to have foiled radicals like Sam Adams and Patrick Henry. And then the East India Company furnished an opportunity for a terrible blunder. Lord North seized the chance.

Bountiful harvests in India had brought the company a tremendous surplus of tea. To unload the ruinous supply, Parliament gave the East India Company new regulations;

27

His Majesty's Privy Councillors insult his most distinguished American subject: Dr. Franklin, who stands quietly before them on January 29, 1774. In London as agent for Massachusetts, he bears the brunt of anger at trouble there. To inflame colonial opinion, Sam Adams had printed copies of high officials' private letters. Returning home, Franklin served in the Continental Congress. Spectacles cherished as a relic lie beside his daughter Sarah's patchbox for silk beauty marks.

PHOTOGRAPHED BY VICTOR R. BOSWELL, JR., NATIONAL GEOGRAPHIC STAFF

even with the Townshend tax its tea would be cheaper than the smugglers'. But Sam Adams claimed that Parliament was trying to bribe Americans. He made the issue as simple as a poster: Tea stood for tyranny!

The first ships of East Indian tea rode at anchor in Boston harbor in December, 1773. Sam Adams demanded that the governor of Massachusetts send the cargo back. The governor refused. With that news, Bostonians masqueraded as Mohawk Indians, boarded the ships, smashed the chests of tea, and —in the words of that onetime moderate John Adams— "3 Cargoes of Bohea Tea were emptied into the Sea. . . . There is a Dignity, a Majesty, Sublimity in this last Effort of the Patriots . . . so bold, so daring . . . an Epocha in History."

"He must have enjoyed seeing them play Indian," Kel remarked.

But others played a different game. George III, deploring "the rebellious disposition which unhappily exists," found biddable friends in Parliament. By lopsided majorities Parliament wrote anger into law: It reorganized the government of Massachusetts to strengthen royal control, and slammed shut the port of Boston. And then it passed the Quebec Act, extending that province south to the Ohio River and pledging toleration for its Roman Catholic subjects. In this measure Americans saw a threat to their western lands—and a lurking menace to their own religious liberty. With these Intolerable Acts, Parliament had lighted a fuse.

If King George hoped to isolate the Boston firebrands from the other colonists, he failed utterly. With typical fervor the ladies of Edenton, North Carolina, gathered to foreswear the drinking of British tea. Among them was one Penelope Barker, who brought tea cakes for a tea-less tea party.

"And Mistress Barker's recipe survives," our friend Mary Ann Harrell told Tina. Mary Ann's mother dug the recipe out of family files and soon Tina was measuring brown sugar and beating eggs.

"Penelope Barker must have been a genius," said Tina, "if she could roll these cookies out thin." But the results were worth it. Before the cookies could cool, Tina ate ten. "Who needs British tea?" she asked.

George Washington and his neighbors made similar remarks in 1774. When Washington celebrated his re-election to the House of Burgesses, an English visitor in Alexandria noted the refreshments: "a Hogshead of Toddy . . . Coffee and Chocolate, but no Tea. This Herb is in disgrace. . . ."

Or perhaps not the herb itself. ". . . Sir, what is it we are contending against? Is it against paying the duty of three pence per pound on tea because burthensome?" asked George Washington of his old friend and neighbor Bryan Fairfax. "No," he said, answering his own question, "it is the right only we have all along disputed. . . ."

But Fairfax was a royalist who greatly feared "continual Broils and Revolutions"

At Mount Vernon on July 4, 1774, George Washington wrote: "I am very much engaged in raising one o

and believed that "the People at Boston were blameable...."

Washington defended "the quiet and steady conduct of the people of the Massachusetts Bay," and warned: "...the crisis is arrived when we must assert our rights, or submit... till custom and use shall make us...tame and abject slaves...."

Somewhat wistfully, Fairfax admitted, "There are scarce any at Alexandria of my opinion." But his argument with Washington was not personal: "...I am convinced that no Man in the Colony...would go greater lengths to serve it, nor is at the same time a better subject to the Crown."

Washington accepted this royal, loyal compliment, then wrote, "I shall set off on Wednesday next for Philadelphia," for George Washington had been chosen a delegate to the First Continental Congress.

Rob in a tricorne chortles at Josh's try for a fox-hunting call on Washington's English-made horn.

...he additions to my house...." Next May he left the mansion unfinished to defend the colonies' rights.

NATIONAL GEOGRAPHIC PHOTOGRAPHERS JOSEPH J. SCHERSCHEL (BELOW) AND JAMES L. STANFIELD

First blood at Lexington: A sudden outburst of firing takes eight American lives. The resolute Minutemen

1775:
"Let It Begin Here"

nswer an unexpected volley from British light infantry, and April 19, 1775, dawns as a day of battle.

WE MADE our family forays only when school permitted, so we followed most of the winter campaigns during Christmas holidays. Under the spell of the season, the youngsters started collecting Christmas stories from the Revolution. Curiously, the last days of each December seemed an augury for the coming year.

On Christmas Day of 1774, for example, we found the most famous living American —Benjamin Franklin—completing his long residence in London as colonial agent and lobbyist. Waiting for a new Parliament to meet,

Franklin pays an evening call to talk politics with Richard, Admiral Lord Howe, at his sister's home. She has voiced her deep concern: "I hope we are not to have civil war."

No one in London, of course, knows what is happening at that moment in the American colonies; ships bring news already three months old. On Christmas Day, 1774, Franklin himself cannot know that his wife Deborah is dead and three days buried during a Philadelphia snowstorm.

In Boston the winter is unusually mild—a

33

fortunate fact, for the port is closed to shipments of firewood as well as other commerce. Homes are chilly. And soon sickness will fill the cemeteries, adding grief to grudge.

On Virginia plantations the traditional Christmas guns noisily boom out a morning Yuletide salute. Young Thomas Jefferson is at Monticello for what he once described as "the day of greatest mirth and jollity." This will be his last Yuletide there for years.

George Washington quietly writes letters at Mount Vernon; house slaves will prepare a room for Col. Charles Lee, the brilliant and slovenly English officer who has thrown in his lot with the colonies. He will arrive in just five days. And how can two veterans avoid guessing the future?

By the light of tallow candles, quill pens are scratching noisily these long December evenings. In Philadelphia, an articulate but still unsuccessful Englishman named Thomas Paine is polishing an essay that will soon be printed, a minor work but a start. In New York City, a King's College student not yet 20 has concluded a bulky tract fully 14,000 words long. "The sacred rights of mankind," he writes, "are not to be rummaged for

among old parchments.... They are written as with a sunbeam, in the whole volume of human nature...." The author does not sign his pamphlet—who would recognize the name of Alexander Hamilton?

Gradually, the measured written words of late 1774 are given voice in the shouts of 1775. The fiery Patrick Henry will soon address his fellow Burgesses and coin his most famous phrase: "Give me liberty or give me death!" And the year 1775 moves on, from pamphlet to shout—toward the shots of war.

PAUL REVERE'S whole hearty life pervades Christ Church of Boston, the Old North Church of tradition. At age 15 young Paul regularly rang these church bells. As a mature silversmith, the square-faced, square-handed artist fashioned a sterling chalice still used here for Holy Communion. Finally, as an old man, he worshiped here in pew number 54.

For a moment, our family sat down in it. Only a nod away was pew number 62, used by King George's last Massachusetts governor, Gen. Thomas Gage. The church was so full of peace that even young Rob fell quiet.

In Old North Church, at exactly three on the afternoon of Easter Tuesday, April 18, 1775, the peace ended for a continent. At that hour patriotic members of the parish met and discharged its loyalist rector, who, as he put it, agreed to "give up the keys and quit the Church"—and just in time.

Within hours these keys were needed to put "two lanthorns in the North Church steeple" as a signal that the British were moving toward Concord by water. We climbed the church tower, spiraling past the bulky bells for a view of Boston rooftops. Louvers filtered away two centuries. An unsettled April sky, like ours today, had also slicked the cobbles and leaden roofs of Boston in 1775.

Bostonians then knew their neighbors—all 15,000 of them, not counting General

"A hurry of hoofs ... a shape in the moonlight, a bulk in the dark...." Longfellow's words gallop again with the Cyrus Dallin statue of Paul Revere in Boston. It stands in twilight silhouette before Christ Church, the Old North Church of history. On April 18, two lanterns—"two, if by sea"—signaled the river route of British troops heading toward Concord to seize a store of munitions. At left, the author's son Kel carries facsimile lanterns up the belfry tower.

Paul Revere slips out of Boston by moonlight; friends row him past H.M.S. Somerset at anchor in the Charles River. He rides hard for Lexington to give the alarm, "The regulars are out!" By midnight he warns two patriot leaders at Parson Jonas Clarke's: Gray-haired Sam Adams questions him while John Hancock, anxious to fight, clutches a musket.

36

Gage's 3,500 troops quartered in the port. Every gossip knew that some 700 of those troops were moving through the night to seize the powder at Concord—were they after the patriot leaders in Lexington? As he later recalled, the volunteer courier Revere "would immediately set off for Lexington, where Messrs. Hancock and Adams were, and acquaint them of the movement. . . ."

Revere's account continues, as direct and plain as his own honest face but with just a glint of the silversmith: "Two friends rowed me across Charles River . . . where the *Somerset* man-of-war lay. It was then young flood, the ship was winding, and the moon was rising. They landed me on the Charlestown side. . . . I got a horse of Deacon Larkin."

And so began the famous ride. We retraced Revere's route for 15 miles. Near Cambridge, he just missed capture, and hurried on to Medford where "I awaked the captain of the minutemen. And after that I alarmed almost every house till I got to Lexington."

Revere made good time, for he hurried past Buckman's Tavern in Lexington about midnight. He found the place restlessly astir with rumors and lights. And when he pulled up his reins at the home of the Reverend Mr. Jonas Clarke, where John Hancock and Sam Adams were resting, Revere found guards warning him that the family had just retired and wanted no noise.

"Noise!" bellowed Revere. "You'll have noise enough before long. The regulars are coming out!"

A springtime romance revised American history that night. Samuel Prescott, a young Concord doctor, had been calling on his Lexington sweetheart, one of the Mulliken girls. The hour grew late. Finally, about 1 a.m. Dr.

"If you go an inch further you are a dead man," swear British officers capturing Revere about three miles beyond Lexington. But his fellow couriers William Dawes and Samuel Prescott escaped; Dr. Prescott galloped on to Concord, and its town bell called the neighborhood to arms.

Prescott headed home — and joined two other Concord-bound riders, Paul Revere and his fellow courier William Dawes, now arrived by way of Boston Neck. The patriot riders recognized the doctor as a "high son of liberty."

But so did a British patrol. As Paul Revere told it, "In an instant, I saw four officers who rode up to me with their pistols in their hands and said, '... stop! If you go an inch further, you are a dead man!' "

Revere was taken prisoner; Dawes, thrown from his horse, escaped on foot through the woods. But Dr. Prescott, who knew this land even in the dark, jumped his horse over a stone wall and reached Concord with the news. Thanks to the charms of moonlight and Miss Mulliken, the patriots finished hiding most of their stores before morning.

By now Lexington had armed itself. Capt. John Parker had mustered 130 Minutemen, all now waiting within earshot of a drum.

Standing by at the sooty hearth of Buckman's Tavern was a tired but excited youth named William Diamond, one of the company's drummer boys. At dawn, a scout brought Captain Parker news that the British were close at hand. As a young Minuteman named Sylvanus Wood wrote, "Parker immediately turned to his drummer ... and ordered him to beat to arms...."

The Minutemen came running, about 70 of them, and formed into two lines on the common beside the road to Concord. The sun rose, striping the April grass with long lines of light and shadow. Then came the scarlet column of British soldiers.

Captain Parker's immortal command is now carved into stone: "Stand your ground; don't fire unless fired upon; but if they mean to have a war, let it begin here!"

The words are certainly brave and possibly true. But at that instant no witness wrote them down.

The British column entered the green — moving head-on toward the Minutemen. Astride his horse was Maj. John Pitcairn of the Royal Marines, the reasonable and the

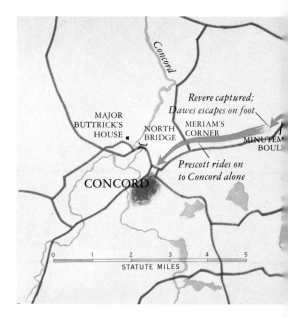

Crunching acorns under hoof, Tina and Josh ride Revere's route along Nelson Road not far from Lexington. Tradition says Josiah Nelson awoke as Revere, Prescott, and Dawes dashed past his home. When Nelson rushed outside, one of the pursuing redcoats slashed him with a saber.

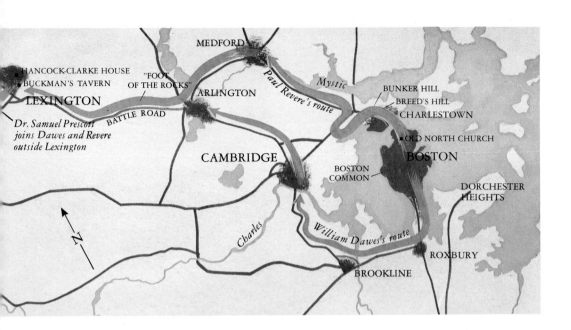

HANCOCK-CLARKE HOUSE
BUCKMAN'S TAVERN
"FOOT OF THE ROCKS"
LEXINGTON
MEDFORD
ARLINGTON
Paul Revere's route
Mystic
BUNKER HILL
BREED'S HILL
CHARLESTOWN
Dr. Samuel Prescott joins Dawes and Revere outside Lexington
BATTLE ROAD
OLD NORTH CHURCH
CAMBRIDGE
BOSTON
BOSTON COMMON
DORCHESTER HEIGHTS
N
Charles
William Dawes's route
ROXBURY
BROOKLINE

NATIONAL GEOGRAPHIC PHOTOGRAPHER WINFIELD PARKS; PORTRAIT AND PISTOLS, LEXINGTON HISTORICAL SOCIETY, INCORPORATED

reasonably popular commander of this first British force, perhaps 180 men.

Standing with his neighbors, Captain Parker made the only sensible choice, ordering his men to scatter "and not to fire." Slowly, the men began to break ranks. They long remembered Major Pitcairn's commands:

"Disperse, ye rebels! Lay down your arms!"

Then a gun was fired. Some witnesses insisted the shot came from a pistol—and British officers carried pistols—but no one knows. Like a brain concussion that erases the memory of the blow that caused it, that first shot echoes unidentified through history.

At once, noise and confusion engulfed the scene—other volleys, shots, British voices cheering in the smoke, and the flash of British bayonets on the charge.

Some Minutemen died instantly—like Jonas Parker, who fired his musket, held his ground, and was stabbed by bayonet while trying to reload. Others were wounded—some lightly, like the one British regular nicked in the leg.

The firing stopped. An east wind cleared the smoke on eight dead and ten wounded Americans. British officers formed up their troops again to march the Concord road.

"... I returned to the Common and.... I assisted in carrying the dead into the meeting house," said Sylvanus Wood. But as he told the story, his grief grew hard: "I then proceeded toward Concord with my gun...."

We followed Sylvanus Wood along the Battle Road, watching Concord willows cast their first veiled tones of April green. And in this

PHOTOGRAPHS BY VICTOR R. BOSWELL, JR., NATIONAL GEOGRAPHIC STAFF

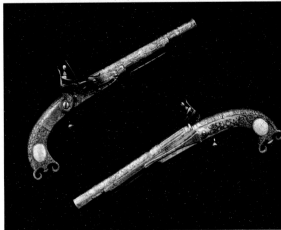

remarkably gentle setting, I showed the children a harsh fragment of history in a copy of the Salem *Essex Gazette* for 1775.

"They misspelled the words!" said Josh, in deep disillusion.

"No," said Kel scornfully, "in those days some of the *s*'s looked like *f*'s."

We read it aloud: "Last Wednesday, the 19th of April, the Troops of his *Britannick* Majesty commenced Hostilities upon the People of this Province.... we are involved in all the Horrors of a civil War...."

"Are you reading the *very same* story," asked Josh, "that the Americans read *then* about the battle?"

The words seemed strangely timeless when read beside the rebuilt Concord bridge. Our reporter had traced the British column of 700

Beside the hearth in Buckman's Tavern, Minutemen of John Parker's Lexington company passed the chilly hours before daybreak, April 19. Then a scout's report sent them running to the green where they met the British and heard the cry, "Throw down your arms, ye villains, ye rebels," perhaps from Maj. John Pitcairn (above), who led the advance unit of redcoats. He always insisted that the "peasants" shot first and his own men fired against orders. Retreating from Concord that same day he lost the silver-mounted pistols when his horse threw him and bolted. At Bunker Hill, less than two months later, Major Pitcairn fell mortally wounded near his own son. His men agreed, "We have all lost a father."

men on "their March for Concord; at which Place they destroyed several Carriages, Carriage Wheels, and about 20 Barrels of Flour, all belonging to the Province. Here about 150 men going towards a Bridge, of which the Enemy were in Possession, the latter fired, and killed 2 of our Men, who then returned the Fire, and obliged the Enemy to retreat back to Lexington...."

Literary folklore clings like moss to every stone on the battle road. We followed it — by car, by saddle horse, even by foot. At Meriam's Corner we took special note; here the firing became intense and veteran Amos Barrett always remembered, "a grait many Lay dead and the Road was bloddy."

Britain's Lord Percy, who brought reinforcements, paid tribute to the Minutemen who fired from the stone walls: "Nor are ... their men void of spirit ... for many of them concealed themselves in houses, & advanced within 10 yds. to fire at me & other officers, tho' they were morally certain of being put to death themselves in an instant."

And so the carnage continued on a battlefield of strange and horrible proportions: 200 yards wide and 16 miles long. Our Salem newspaper correspondent reported it well: "The Enemy.... continued their Retreat from Lexington to Charlestown with great Precipitation; and ... our People continued the Pursuit, firing at them till they got to Charlestown Neck, (which they reached a little after Sunset)...."

The warriors counted their losses: among the British troops, 73 killed and 200 wounded or missing; and among the Americans, 49 dead, 46 wounded, and 5 missing. So, sealed in blood, resistance turned to rebellion. As surviving diaries show, everyone seemed

LINE OF THE MINUTE MEN
APRIL 9   1775
STAND YOUR GROUND
DON'T FIRE UNLESS FIRED UPON
BUT IF THEY MEAN TO HAVE A WAR
LET IT BEGIN HERE
CAPTAIN PARKER

Jonathan Harrington's anguished wife tries to aid her wounded husband in this 1859 engraving of Lexington. Actually Harrington dragged himself to the door of his home, where she saw him die. Here, contrary to fact, a spirited defense claims two redcoats. Today a boulder marks the line where the Minutemen stood at their captain's legendary order, and muskets from the Revolution still thunder in annual celebrations.

to realize the heavy history of the day.

"Oh, what a glorious morning is this!" exulted Sam Adams when he heard from two miles away the shots in Lexington.

To the rhythm of galloping hoofs, the news moved along colonial post roads. Accounts of the battle were printed on April 25 in Philadelphia, April 27 in both New York and Baltimore, May 9 in Charleston, and May 31 in Savannah. Eventually, the news reached all the 37 newspapers then printed in the 13 colonies. Readers passed them from hand to hand and hungered for still more details.

From Philadelphia, where he was attending the Continental Congress, George Washington pieced together his own "Account of the engagement in the Massachusetts Bay." In a letter to a friend, he carefully called the British regulars "the Ministerial Troops ... for we do not, nor cannot yet prevail upon ourselves to call them the King's Troops.... Unhappy it is ... to reflect, that a Brother's Sword has been sheathed in a Brother's breast.... But can a virtuous Man hesitate in his choice?"

We also sifted through the battle lore. The youngsters saw the house in Arlington where 12 American Minutemen were killed. They took the measure of Charlestown Neck, crossed by those British soldiers who had marched nearly 40 miles in one day. Each

43

one of us found a story with a special appeal.

Martha prefers a story told by the wife of a Minuteman: "Isaac Davis... was my husband. He was then thirty years of age. We had four children; the youngest about fifteen months old. They were all unwell when he left me, in the morning; some of them with the canker-rash.

"The alarm was given early in the morning, and my husband lost no time in making ready to go to Concord with his company.... My husband said but little that morning. He seemed serious and thoughtful; but never seemed to hesitate.... He only said, 'Take good care of the children,' and was soon out of sight.

"In the afternoon he was brought home a corpse. He was placed in my bedroom till the funeral."

And each of the 49 American dead left some such legacy.

Modern townsfolk in Concord and Lexington observe Patriots' Day each year on April 19 with a parade of Minutemen and musicians. Naturally, youngsters love it. During the Concord parade, Josh turned to me and asked, "Next year in music class could I study the fife?"

But it was Rob who surprised us all. In the car he began to hum and drum. "That's 'Yankee Doodle'!" Tina shrieked. "Rob can actually carry the tune!"

So he could, for that jaunty air is easily caught and carried. I carefully explained to Rob that his new tune was really a prize of war. The British regulars had long used "Yankee Doodle" as an insult, for the title had come to mean a country bumpkin or hick. At least one meeting of Boston patriots had been broken up when the British noisily played this tune. On the morning of April 19, 1775, Lord Percy's fifes and drums had

A post rider carried the battle news to New Haven, Connecticut. There a local militia commander, a druggist-merchant named Benedict Arnold, lost no time. He demanded keys to the powder house, and when he was refused by town officials, he shouted, "None but Almighty God shall prevent my marching!" He threatened to batter down the door, and the officials relented.

Then, as his 50 men marched off for Cambridge, Captain Arnold got an idea—the patriots besieging Boston badly needed cannon. Cannon! As a horse-trader, Arnold had often journeyed to Quebec and passed that rotting relic of the French and Indian War, Fort Ticonderoga. What a prize its large store of scarce artillery would be. And what a bold strategic stroke! In patriot hands, Fort Ti could command Lake Champlain and block the road of British regulars coming down from Canada.

Arnold suggested the idea, and the Massachusetts Committee of Safety at once gave him the assignment. But Connecticut authorities had meantime handed the same job to another party: Ethan Allen and his Green Mountain Boys. Uneasily, the men shared command. A quarrel was inevitable.

"Why couldn't they get along?" asked Josh, as we drove up the Hudson valley. I tried to explain how men from Vermont ("Vermont means 'green mountain'") might resent a stranger from Connecticut. But I think it was the scenery itself that finally dramatized the point. Like Arnold and Allen, we were making this trip in early May when nights are cold and steam rises from the streams in early morning and the trees look naked in the springtime sun. We climbed, rounded a turn — and a spacious view opened up.

"Wow!" said Josh. "Are these mountains the Rockies?"

These were the Adirondacks, but the scenery at least had the bigness of the wide Wild West. And from that moment on, Josh had some notion of Ethan Allen's friends: rough, tough frontiersmen at least half-outlaw, led by the roughest and loudest of them all.

played the same impudent piece on their way toward Lexington.

The heat of battle had soured the joke. One American diarist described the way the exhausted British finally "intrenched for the Night upon Bunker Hill after having danced the tune of Yankee Doodle...." Whatever else they had won that day, the Minutemen had captured "Yankee Doodle."

And so I explained how this taunt turned into a tribute, and eventually became our national nickname. Rob thought about the story for a moment.

"I know who started the war," he said with great assurance. "It was the Yankee Doodle drummer boy."

Rob had scrambled the images: Lord Percy's fifes and William Diamond's long roll. But he had at least caught the rising cadence of war's drumbeat and the quickstep of a nation-still-to-be.

Like many mountain people, Allen was a fascinating personality. Part theologian, part roustabout, he could command rich oaths and even richer Old Testament eloquence.

Before dawn on May 10, 1775, an unlikely party approached the sleeping Fort Ticonderoga by boat and rushed through an open gate. With Arnold entering beside him, Ethan Allen demanded the surrender of the 45-man garrison. Some say he shouted, "Come out you damned old rat!" But Allen recalled the surrender with differing detail:

"... The capt. came immediately to the door with his breeches in his hand ... I ordered him to deliver me the fort instantly ... 'In the name of the great Jehovah and the Continental Congress.'"

In ten bloodless minutes, the Americans took Ticonderoga, its artillery, tons of lead shot, and 30,000 flints.

TWO WEEKS and one day after the fall of Ticonderoga, the British frigate *Cerberus* dropped anchor in Boston harbor. Even the name of the vessel seemed "an odd circumstance" to a Virginia editor, since Cerberus was "the three-headed dog that guards the mouth of hell" and now this ship of war had brought "the three generals appointed to tame the Americans."

The senior general was William Howe, a big, tight-lipped, high-living professional soldier with a special interest in light infantry. He was the brother of Franklin's friend Lord Howe and himself a member of Parliament; only a few months before, he had promised the voters that he would refuse a command against the Americans.

Standing beside Howe, Maj. Gen. Henry Clinton seemed short, dumpy, distant, and shy; he was a capable soldier though unlucky and suspicious. What Clinton lacked in dash, the third general supplied amply: John Burgoyne, "handsome Jack" to his contempo-

raries, once colonel of the 16th Light Dragoons. For a dozen years, Burgoyne had served in the House of Commons, inspiring gossip, and playing at cards and cups and amateur acting. The great David Garrick, in fact, had recently staged Burgoyne's first drama in London.

And so the three heads from *Cerberus* came ashore to Boston town with British reinforcements. The generals peered at the improvised armies that ringed the port, and Burgoyne pronounced a need to "make elbow room." As the weather and tempers grew hotter, they urged Gage to take action.

Temperatures were also rising in Philadelphia. A muggy heat wave had hit the city just as delegations arrived for the Continental Congress. Now with its brick and pavement, the city seemed uncomfortably crowded—and was. Some 40,000 residents made Philadelphia the greatest city in British North America—vying for second largest in the whole English-speaking world.

The times were martial. The Continental Congress—virtually the same body that had affirmed its loyalty to the king the previous autumn—needed to adopt the volunteer farmers' army in front of Boston. It had to find ammunition and food to keep that army in the field. "Coll. Washington appears at Congress in his Uniform," reported John Adams on May 29, "and, by his great Experience ... in military Matters, is of much service to Us."

And then, on June 14, John Adams rose and proposed that Congress appoint a commander-in-chief, praising "a Gentleman from Virginia who ..."

While Adams thus delivered his Man-Who speech, Washington himself "from his usual Modesty darted into the Library Room," as Adams later recalled. Cousin Sam Adams seconded the motion; the election was unanimous; and so leadership moved from agitators and orators to another kind of man.

But what kind? Thomas Jefferson, who had served with Washington as a Burgess at Williamsburg, could not recall ever hearing him "speak ten minutes at a time, nor to any but the main point which was to decide the question."

He was quiet. Yet everyone noticed him. In an age when most men were short, Washington stood six feet two, massively muscled, big boned; he weighed about 200 pounds. He was a gentleman, well accustomed to

Minuteman in bronze keeps a timeless guard over North Bridge, from the spot where the "embattled farmers" of 1775 "fired the shot heard round the world." Ralph Waldo Emerson's words immortalize the Americans' first deliberate attack on their king's forces. Within moments the regulars fled. Their desperate retreat toward Boston lasted from midday until twilight under a galling fire, along the route known today as the Battle Road.

command, a poised, urbane planter. But not effete. Since his youth, he had known how to move through frontier forests, how to treat with Indians, how to fight and how to live. He was a man's man.

He came from the South, and the New England farmers ringing Boston needed continent-wide support. He had commanded a regiment on the frontier for five years. And George Washington also had a feeling for the shape of the land, had surveyed it with precision, explored and mapped it, speculated in it, tilled it, loved it. Soon he would learn how to fortify and defend it.

He brought other qualities that we can sense now in the unaffected, moving letter he wrote his "dear Patsy," as he called Martha Washington, breaking the momentous news: "It has been determined in Congress, that the whole army raised for the defence of the

British regulars, shamed and tired, march into some of the day's bloodiest fighting as they pass "Foot of the Rocks." Their flank guards try to defend the column as hundreds of militiamen swarm to the attack, many carrying guns made for duck-shooting. Above, Josh McDowell takes aim from the cleft in Minuteman Boulder where an earlier marksman brought down two redcoats.

49

American cause shall be put under my care. ... so far from seeking this appointment, I have used every endeavor in my power to avoid it ... a trust too great for my capacity. ... But as it has been a kind of destiny, that has thrown me upon this service, I shall hope that my undertaking it is designed to answer some good purpose.... As life is always uncertain ... I got Colonel Pendleton to draft a will for me...." He signed himself "Yr affecte Go Washington."

On that quiet Philadelphia Sunday, doubting himself but not his cause, the general had no way of knowing what had happened only the day before in Massachusetts. On the road to Boston he would learn of Bunker Hill.

BEFORE I TOOK MY FAMILY to visit the Bunker Hill battlefield, we made an expedition to the twenty-sixth floor of a Boston skyscraper named for John Hancock. The day was clear and our view was a lesson in both geography and the military arts.

"I wonder if that harbor still has chests of tea on the bottom," said Josh, who then wanted to be an underwater photographer. We could clearly see the changes of two centuries — bridges, freeways, big buildings — and beneath such progress, the old geography: Boston stood on a jutting thumb of land; and this thumb almost touched the finger that was Charlestown, about a mile away across the Charles River estuary.

The Bunker Hill monument, a tall obelisk, stands out among the factory smokestacks of Charlestown. From our distance, it was easy to imagine earthworks on the two steep rises: Breed's Hill and — a bit taller and farther northwest — Bunker Hill. We could see how guns on those heights could bombard the town and ships in the harbor.

Leaders of the patriot army reached the same conclusion. On the night of June 16, 1775, some 1,200 Americans moved out with picks, shovels, and guns to build and hold a redoubt. They crossed over the 110-foot height of Bunker Hill, then dipped over to the 75-foot crest of Breed's. Throughout the night, they worked.

By the first light of Saturday, June 17, British sentries were startled to see raw, unfinished fortifications crowning Breed's Hill.

His Majesty's ships opened fire at them, and early in the afternoon the Americans saw 28 barges of British regulars moving across the water. Brave and assured, Gen. William Howe was coming to take Breed's Hill. He personally commanded the British right flank.

"Our troops advanced with great confidence," one British officer remembered later. "... As we approached, an incessant stream of fire poured from the rebel lines.... for near thirty minutes."

Here was the crux of it: The British expected an 18th-century textbook response — an inaccurate volley of American musket fire, followed by panic and retreat. Instead, the redcoats met surprise.

"Don't fire until you see the whites of their eyes," the old ranger Israel Putnam had shouted as he rode the American lines on his horse. Others yelled it, too. "Fire low.... Every one of you can kill a squirrel at a hundred yards .... Pick off the commanders."

Squirrels weren't usually killed that way by a Brown Bess musket, the standard weapon in those days. Kel once examined a Brown Bess in a museum. "Nearly five feet long!" he marveled as he hefted it.

We looked up its performance record in an 18th-century book and found that the musket "if not exceedingly ill bored ... will strike a man at eighty yards; it may even at 100."

"That's the length of a football field," Kel translated. "And an M-1 kills at ten times that range." But at close quarters the spherical one-ounce musket ball was a terrible, tearing thing. It stopped a man, splintered bone, ripped the vitals.

And this cruel truth New Hampshireman John Stark well knew. In front of his barricade beside the Mystic River, 96 British regulars fell dead. "I never saw sheep lie as thick in the fold," said Stark grimly.

British regulars retreated toward their boats. They drew back from the hill itself, reformed, tried again. Then for the second time, the regulars fell back.

Watching the disorder, General Howe

Civilian in uniform, Washington leaves a session of the First Continental Congress, meeting in Carpenters' Hall at Philadelphia in 1774. He wears a colonel's garb from the French and Indian War; at his side walks Patrick Henry with Richard Henry Lee, also attending from Virginia. Scholars now think Washington put on militia blue in May, 1775, to indicate his mood as delegates talked of peace — and prepared for war.

General Washington assumes command of the Grand Army of the United Colonies on July 2 under a Cambridge elm, a favorite theme for many 19th-century artists. In fact, however, he arrived unannounced, probably without ceremony. Perhaps a few idle troops gave him a salute as he rode past the Yard at Harvard College (left) on a Sunday afternoon.

faced *"A moment that I never felt before."* Scholars and warriors would long study that moment and measure its effect on Howe and the whole war. But on that hot day the spectacle overshadowed its results.

When the British set fire to Charlestown to clear it of snipers, Gen. John Burgoyne watched intently from across the Charles River; he wrote this wide-screen scenario for a nephew in England: "... They were ... exceedingly hurt by musketry from Charlestown.... Howe sent us word by a boat and desired us to set fire to the town, which was immediately done....

"... now ensued one of the greatest scenes of war that can be conceived. If we look to the height, Howe's corps ascending the hill in the face of the entrenchments and ... much engaged. To the left the enemy pouring in fresh troops ... and in the arm of the sea our ships and floating batteries cannonading them. Straight before us, a large and noble town in one great blaze. The church steeples being of timber were great pyramids of fire above the rest...."

General Howe was making his third hard try against Breed's Hill.

Even before the battle, the farmers' army had felt "almost beat out," as one of them recalled, "being tired by our labor and having

no sleep the night before, but little victuals, no drink but rum."

But with a dry mouth one old man prayed loud enough for his compatriots to hear him in the redoubt, "I thank thee, O Lord, for sparing me to fight this day."

The patriot Col. William Prescott and his 150 men continued to endure "a very smart firing on both sides," as Prescott reported, before he found "our ammunition...nearly exhausted." Prescott retreated, using his sword to parry British bayonets.

Not all were spared for that retreat. Dr. Joseph Warren, just three days a major general by vote of the Provincial Congress, fell dead with a bullet behind his ear.

As he squeezed off his last shot, Caesar Bason was wounded in the thigh. Bason was a powerful man—one of the free Negroes who chose to fight on Breed's Hill that day. Bleeding profusely, he ducked behind a stone wall and fell, too weak to walk. But with Capt. Aaron Smith and more shot, he fought on. The two Americans worked by a load-and-fire system until Smith's gun was smashed and the British swept the hill.

General Howe did not pursue the patriots.

They had other forces around Cambridge, and his own men, as he wrote, were "so much harrassed." All night the streets of Boston echoed to the sounds of carriages and litters bearing back the wounded and dead. "A dear bought victory," said General Clinton; "another such would have ruined us." And right he was, for 1,054 Britons fell that Saturday in what is called the Battle of Bunker Hill; at least 226 died. The Americans reckoned their loss at 30 captured, 271 wounded, and 140 killed.

"Is that really a lot?" asked Tina, accustomed to the numerals of another century. I assured her that for the British, Bunker Hill was the costliest battle in the eight-year war.

One of the fallen was Maj. John Pitcairn, carried from the Charlestown slopes by his own son. We had already seen his captured Scottish pistols on display in Lexington. Now we read his name carved on a stone crypt.

"That's the same Major Pitcairn who brought the redcoats to Lexington?" asked Josh. It was. For the major is interred—with justice, Christian respect, and irony—beneath Boston's Old North Church.

The greatest casualty of Bunker Hill was

53

the myth of Yankee cowardice. Mild General Gage was profoundly shocked at the "Rage and Enthousiasm, as great as ever People were possessed of.... *I wish this Cursed place was burned!"*

In London friends of George III concurred. The news of Bunker Hill sped home in a swift 38 days. Peace-loving Lord North wavered, considered the casualties, and saw that the uprising was indeed organized; it must be treated as a foreign war. The king agreed. His Proclamation of Rebellion spread the blame wide to "divers parts of our Colonies and Plantations in North America." All his subjects were "bound by Law... to disclose ... all traitorous Conspiracies... against us, our Crown and Dignity...."

General Washington learned about the battle on his way to Boston before entering New York. The dispatch warned that 1,000 enemy casualties "exceeds every other estimation." A greater concern was the powder shortage in Cambridge. But Washington, with a plume in his hat, masked his worries and entered New York, second largest city of the United Colonies with its 22,000 residents.

By a quirk of history, New York greeted the old and the new on the same day, Sunday, June 25: the royal governor William Tryon, returning from 14 months in Britain, and the Congress's general, George Washington,

headed for troubled Massachusetts. The genuinely divided city offered a curious mix of drama, danger, and humor. The *Pennsylvania Journal* reported that Washington drew "a greater number of the principal inhabitants."

WITHOUT EVEN a welcoming committee, General Washington arrived in Cambridge on a rainy July 2, 1775, and took over a bagatelle army. No one even knew its size. Washington's first orders were for a complete muster; and it took a full week—a delay due to "imperfect obedience," thought the general—to learn that only 13,745 men were fit for duty, and they had "not more than 9 cartridges a Man." (British regulars carried 60 cartridges apiece.) From the days of his Virginia regiment, George Washington remembered the military maxim: "Discipline is the soul of an Army." In this army he could see no soul. Officers seemed eager to "curry favor with the men," wrote Washington, "... by whom they were chosen, and on whose smiles possibly they may... again rely."

Washington was far from Virginia, and in shock he referred to his Massachusetts troops as "exceeding dirty and nasty people...."

What were the army encampments like? We're in the debt of the Reverend Mr. William Emerson from Concord, grandfather of Ralph Waldo Emerson, for this description

Charles Thomson, called "the life of the cause of liberty" before the war, served as secretary to the Continental Congress for its 15-year lifetime. Its grateful delegates gave him this silver urn, honoring his fidelity in keeping official journals and secrets. He retired in 1789 and spent 25 peaceful years at Harriton (right), his country home near Philadelphia.

FORT TICONDEROGA MUSEUM (BELOW) AND NATIONAL GEOGRAPHIC PHOTOGRAPHER EMORY KRISTOF

of the camps, "as different in their form as the owners are in their dress.... Some are made of boards, some of sailcloth.... Others are made of stone and turf, and others again of birch and others brush...."

Discipline was now tightened with the whipping post and lashes "upon the bare back." Other prisoners were sentenced "to ride the wooden Horse, fifteen minutes." (I tried the latter punishment briefly once: The wooden horse was a high sawhorse of sorts. Men rode it with feet adangle and weighted. Even without weights, I cannot recommend the wooden horse.)

While Washington tightened up the rank and file, he also examined the commissions for general officers that Congress had handed him: four major generals, eight brigadier generals, and an adjutant general—mostly aging heroes. Of them all, only three men were younger than Washington himself, and one—the great old gunsmith Seth Pomeroy—declined the commission in the ripeness of his seventieth year. At least one of them was virtually illiterate.

When I recited their names to Tina, she stopped me short. "Not so fast!" she pleaded. "How can I tell all these generals apart?"

Washington, I think, had the same problem in those first weeks. Gradually he sorted out the varied faces and accents and backgrounds. Charles Lee and Philip Schuyler, two of his major generals, had accompanied him from Philadelphia. If Lee was, as Abigail Adams called him, "a careless hardy Veteran," he also had great wit and a convincing self-confidence. Kel remembered him as "the dog man," a fellow always followed by "my honest quadruped friends," as Lee called his pets.

Schuyler was totally different: tall, flawlessly dressed, an aristocrat of Dutch descent. He owned great farmlands and forests along the Hudson. Washington sent him north to defend the colony of New York.

Adjutant General Horatio Gates, with

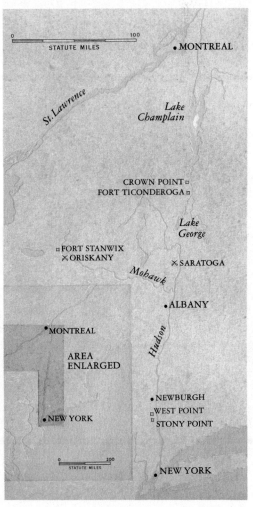

Invasion route of colonial wars, Lake Champlain stretches north 107 miles to Canada. From the promontory, guns of star-shaped Fort Ticonderoga controlled the passage south to Lake George. In a dawn raid on May 10, Ethan Allen dumbfounded a British officer by demanding the fort, as the Vermonter phrased it later, "in the name of the great Jehovah and the Continental Congress."

57

brigadier's rank, an old comrade from the Braddock campaign, helped bring order to the Cambridge administration.

And then there was Nathanael Greene, a strong young Rhode Islander with a stiff knee. He was sensitive about his limp, for it had cost him command of the Rhode Island Kentish Guards. Who wanted an officer who hobbled on review? But Nathanael Greene —a merchant, formerly a Quaker, and son of a prosperous iron foundryman—selflessly served in the ranks, carrying a musket as a private. Later, when his abilities were recognized, he rose from private to general in one long, limping step.

Riding on the road to Roxbury for an inspection of defenses, Washington met a big young man named Henry Knox. The strapping giant was just 25 and had been a Boston bookseller until a few weeks before. Now Knox was applying his book-learning in matters of artillery, engineering, and other military arts. "Knox, the Little Ox," people might have called him, referring to his bulk but foretelling the burdens he would carry.

So Washington took the measure of men and efforts. Large plans were simmering in the late summer heat. Benedict Arnold and Ethan Allen both wanted to invade Canada and had made separate—quite separate— suggestions. Washington had heard of a route through the wilderness "to penetrate into Canada by Way of Kennebeck River, and so to Quebeck." Congress planned an attack on Montreal and Washington added an expedition against Quebec; if the patriots could carry

Fort Ti, rebuilt in this century from utter ruin, flaunts the flags of its captors: French regiments, Britain, and the United Colonies, whose Grand Union banner combined the Union Jack and 13 stripes. Each in turn goes down with the sun.

out this pincer movement, Canada would become the fourteenth rebellious colony.

The project was full of danger: an unmapped frontier, Indians of doubtful alliance, the tempers of Canada's varied residents—some 5,000 speaking English, perhaps 80,000 French. The greatest threat was weather; wrote Washington: "Not a Moments Time is to be lost in the Preparations...."

One army formed in northern New York to advance up Lake Champlain and the Richelieu River to Montreal. General Schuyler started collecting men, among them Ethan Allen. Then Schuyler fell seriously ill with "a billious fever" and turned back, leaving the command of some 2,300 men to his brigadier Richard Montgomery. A well-born Briton, Montgomery had been trained in His Majesty's army, had married a New York Livingston, and taken up the cause of his adopted land. In the remaining weeks of 1775, Montgomery became a hero.

More heroism was a-making on the Kennebec. Arnold, now a colonel, led the 1,000-man force—by sea and river as far as modern Augusta, Maine, and then by batteaux and foot. Dean of Arnold's riflemen was Daniel Morgan, Virginia teamster and veteran of the French and Indian War. He was scantily schooled, but as fine a woodsman as had ever picked his way beyond the Blue Ridge. "Morgan was a large, strong bodied personage," recalled Joseph Henry, who made the Quebec march as a youth. "His manners were of the severest cast; but... he was kind and truly affectionate."

Like his men, Morgan "bore a rifle-barreled gun, a tomahawk,... a 'scalping knife,' which served for all purposes in the woods." And he wore "a deep ash-colored hunting shirt." Whenever he stripped it off, his men could see old scars from a British lash—a punishment that Dan Morgan still hated and would not use. He didn't need a lash, this natural

Checking a restive horse and royal officers as a crowd cheers him on, New York patriot Marinus Willett seizes arms meant for the British in Boston. Within five months, New Yorkers and other colonists read the king's call for all good subjects to help put down the rebellion.

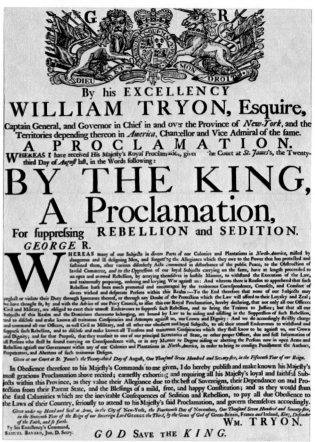

By his EXCELLENCY

WILLIAM TRYON, Esquire,

Captain General, and Governor in Chief in and over the Province of *New-York*, and the Territories depending thereon in *America*, Chancellor and Vice Admiral of the same.

A PROCLAMATION.

WHEREAS I have received His Majesty's Royal Proclamation, given the Court at St. *James*'s, the Twenty-third Day of *August* last, in the Words following:

BY THE KING,
A Proclamation,

For suppressing REBELLION and SEDITION.

GEORGE R.

WHEREAS many of our Subjects in divers Parts of our Colonies and Plantations in *North-America*, misled by dangerous and ill designing Men, and forgetting the Allegiance which they owe to the Power that has protected and sustained them, after various disorderly Acts committed in disturbance of the public Peace, to the Obstruction of lawful Commerce, and to the Oppression of our loyal Subjects carrying on the same, have at length proceeded to an open and avowed Rebellion, by arraying themselves in hostile Manner, to withstand the Execution of the Law, and traitorously preparing, ordering and levying War against us: And whereas there is Reason to apprehend that such Rebellion hath been much promoted and encouraged by the traitorous Correspondence, Counsels, and Comfort of divers wicked and desperate Persons within this Realm.—To the End therefore that none of our Subjects may neglect or violate their Duty through Ignorance thereof, or through any Doubt of the Protection which the Law will afford to their Loyalty and Zeal; we have thought fit, by and with the Advice of our Privy Council, to issue this our Royal Proclamation, hereby declaring, that not only all our Officers Civil and Military, are obliged to exert their utmost Endeavours to suppress such Rebellion, and to bring the Traitors to Justice; but that all our Subjects of this Realm and the Dominions thereunto belonging, are bound by Law to be aiding and assisting in the Suppression of such Rebellion, and to disclose and make known all traitorous Conspiracies and Attempts against us, our Crown and Dignity: And we do accordingly strictly charge and command all our Officers, as well Civil as Military, and all other our obedient and loyal Subjects, to use their utmost Endeavours to withstand and suppress such Rebellion, and to disclose and make known all Treasons and traitorous Conspiracies which they shall know to be against us, our Crown and Dignity; and for that Purpose, that they transmit to one of our principal Secretaries of State, or other proper Officer, due and full Information of all Persons who shall be found carrying on Correspondence with, or in any Manner or Degree aiding or abetting the Persons now in open Arms and Rebellion against our Government within any of our Colonies and Plantations in *North-America*, in order to bring to condign Punishment the Authors, Perpetrators, and Abettors of such traitorous Designs.

Given at our Court at St. James's the Twenty-third Day of August, One Thousand Seven Hundred and Seventy-five, in the Fifteenth Year of our Reign.

In Obedience therefore to his Majesty's Commands to me given, I do hereby publish and make known his Majesty's most gracious Proclamation above recited; earnestly exhorting and requiring all his Majesty's loyal and faithful Subjects within this Province, as they value their Allegiance due to the best of Sovereigns, their Dependance on and Protection from their Parent State, and the Blessings of a mild, free, and happy Constitution; and as they would shun the fatal Calamities which are the inevitable Consequences of Sedition and Rebellion, to pay all due Obedience to the Laws of their Country, seriously to attend to his Majesty's said Proclamation, and govern themselves accordingly.

Given under my Hand and Seal at Arms, in the City of New-York, the Fourteenth Day of November, One Thousand Seven Hundred and Seventy-five, in the Sixteenth Year of the Reign of our Sovereign Lord GEORGE the Third, by the Grace of God of Great-Britain, France and Ireland, King, Defender of the Faith, and so forth.

WM. TRYON.

By his Excellency's Command,
SAMUEL BAYARD, Jun. D. Secry.

GOD SAVE THE *KING*.

leader of men; he set a super-example and pulled followers along with his own vitality.

Arnold, relying on bad maps, had guessed the distance at 180 miles—a journey of less than three weeks. Instead, his army traveled 350 miles in 46 days: a military march that ranks with the epics. The Kennebec, for all its rapids, was the easiest passage. Farther north along the Dead River and the Chaudière came the real test of manhood. One unit turned back and took the provisions of others with them.

Dr. Isaac Senter wrote that "Pork ... the only meat ... would not have been an ounce per man...." Yet, with wonder, the young physician described the way starving men "passed over several rocky mountains, and monstrous precipices ... fired with more than Hannibalian enthusiasm...."

By Wednesday, November 1, the doctor noted: "Our greatest luxuries now consisted in a little water, stiffened with flour, in imitation of shoemakers' paste.... In company was a poor dog ... [who] became a prey for the sustenance of the assassinators. This poor animal was instantly devoured, without leaving any vestige of the sacrifice. Nor did the shaving soap, ... leather of their shoes, cartridge boxes, etc., share any better fate." Next day, when Arnold's band of—now—600 men emerged from the wilderness, "We sat down, eat our rations, blessed our stars," wrote Dr. Senter of his first meal. They reached the chill banks of the St. Lawrence by November 10, camped near the walls of Quebec, and awaited word from Montgomery at the gates of Montreal.

When that news came, it was good: Montgomery captured winter clothing along with Montreal. True, Canada's governor, Gen. Guy

Carleton, escaped by river to Quebec. The governor, in the thick of his troubles, could take some consolation from the fate of Ethan Allen, who had attempted to capture Montreal ahead of Montgomery — and had himself been taken prisoner.

And now Montgomery brought the action downstream along the St. Lawrence to Quebec, where Arnold plotted a way to take what he called "this proud town."

Our whole family followed the Americans to proud Quebec in its appropriate season. A December blizzard had grounded all planes, so we arrived by train — and at night — in a swirling snowstorm.

"Just the kind of night General Montgomery wanted," said Kel, "to mask his attack." More than that, the railroad had brought us into Quebec along the St. Lawrence banks, on the lower shelf of this split-level city. This was the way our compatriots had planned as a battle route.

"We want to make a quick circle," I told our cab driver, "to see a bit of the Lower Town and then go up by Mountain Hill."

In the sparkling blur of snowflakes, Quebec was again the old fortress city, its lower outposts nestling on the riverbank, its haughty citadel perched 300 feet high upon a horseshoe cliff. Snow chains on our cab made a sleighbell sound as we circled through the Lower Town; my eye caught a street sign: Sault-au-Matelot.

"That means Sailor's Jump," said the driver. "Long ago the docks stood here, and sailors jumped ashore on this street."

But the name meant even more. This was the street taken by Arnold and his men when they tried to storm Quebec. General Montgomery's group was to advance along the

61

A panoramic view southward from above Bunker Hill sums up the battle of June 17. On the Charlestown peninsula, the patriots hold the fence (A) from the Mystic River beach to the road. Three flèches (V-shaped earthworks, center) guard the gap between the fence and breastworks leading to the redoubt (B) on the crest of Breed's Hill. About midday, British warships in the Charles and the battery (C) beyond them in distant Boston open a bombardment to cover the barges (D) ferrying Gen. Howe's regiments. Shattered at close range on the Mystic beach (E), his light infantry fails to turn the American flank. Howe leads his men against the fence while his brigadier Robert Pigot assails the redoubt. His reinforcements cross the road at center as Charlestown burns, set afire to drive out rebel snipers. The New Englanders' stand ended with their ammunition; they retreated along the slope at right. The British won the hill at fearful cost; now the Empire faced full-scale war.

PAINTED FOR NATIONAL GEOGRAPHIC BY RICHARD SCHLECHT

southeastern bank on the other side of the city. The American forceps would close beneath the cliff where a street led to Mountain Hill Gate. Arnold and Montgomery would enter Upper Town and secure their prize.

But British General Carleton and his 1,800 defenders knew what was coming. Montgomery himself was prepared for "melancholy consequences." In the same dark mood, Capt. Jacob Cheeseman even put five gold pieces in his pocket, "sufficient to bury him with decency." And as in some terrible fable, all the forebodings came true.

About 2 a.m. of New Year's Eve an overcast sky worsened, and the two groups began their pincer movement along the banks.

"The storm was outrageous," remembered

Daring the odds of British cannon, Col. William Prescott strolls the parapet of his redoubt on Breed's Hill to calm his uneasy men. Awaiting attack, they strengthen their earthworks under heavy bombardment from the ships in the Charles.

Tramping past dead and wounded comrades, the regulars march steadily up Breed's Hill for another assault on the armed American civilians in the redoubt. Eyes front, they see the scarlet litter left by rebel bullets at close range, with the same fate awaiting most of them. Prescott's farmers hold their fire till they see the sweat gleaming on enemy faces, then loose a volley that leaves survivors scattered but undaunted. Stripped to shirtsleeves, the British made a last grim charge and took the hill as its defenders ran out of powder.

PAINTING BY F. C. YOHN, CIRCA 1910, THE CONTINENTAL INSURANCE COMPANY

"THE BATTLE OF BUNKER'S HILL" BY JOHN TRUMBULL, 1786, YALE UNIVERSITY ART GALLERY

Joseph Henry, who was with Arnold's party. "When we came near . . . Palace gate, a horrible roar of cannon took place, and a ringing of all the bells of the city. . . . Arnold . . . advanced perhaps one hundred yards before the main body. . . ."

On the cliffy ramparts just above the Sailor's Jump and from nearby houses, Carleton's men fired their muskets down on Arnold's corps. I perched on the same ramparts to see the spot where Arnold fell, a bullet in his left leg. That one shot helped save Quebec for George III: Arnold's men faltered, time spilled away, opportunity vanished before Morgan led them on.

Beside the St. Lawrence, below Cape

Diamond, a single cannon blast now beheaded the whole American campaign. Just as General Montgomery shouted, "Come on, my good soldiers. . . ." grapeshot struck him down. Montgomery died instantly and with him, Captain Cheeseman. Demoralized, the Americans retreated.

And so the big old teamster Daniel Morgan found himself at bay, hopelessly surrounded in the strange city; but Morgan refused to surrender his sword, even when ordered at gunpoint. Instead, he rushed into a crowd and handed his sword to a startled priest so "these cowards shall not take it. . . ." Morgan, like 425 other rebel Americans, became Guy Carleton's prisoner.

American prisoners were held. "One of your Americans tried to escape from a window there," said the Abbé Honorius Provost, Seminary archivist.

"The prisoners were the lucky ones," said Maj. Georges Guimond, the retired director of the military museum in the Citadel. And the major was quite right. The wounded Arnold and the others who continued the siege suffered bleakly through the winter. Smallpox appeared and finally reached the stage of an epidemic.

When the ice broke up in the river and the Royal Navy could reinforce Carleton, the Americans retreated homeward, having endured greater privations than those they besieged. Others, of course, never returned.

"In 1956 we did some digging near the St. Louis gate," said Major Guimond. "And we uncovered some human bones — probably the grave of Captain Cheeseman. I got our engineers to make a solid box well lined with tin so that we could rebury the captain properly where he had lain." So, thanks to a Canadian soldier, Captain Cheeseman indeed received — twice over — the "decent burial" he wanted.

Our snowstorm ended, and New Year's Day dawned bright. Momentarily all of us retreated from the 18th century and Quebec itself — adjourning to the ski slopes nearby. All went well until a young man from the ski patrol came up to me quickly and asked, "Are you Monsieur McDowell, father of the injured child?"

It was Josh. He had twisted his knee painfully and needed X-rays at the hospital L'Hôtel-Dieu de Québec. We rushed to the emergency room.

While a doctor and a beatific nun wheeled Josh off for his tests, I waited, killing time with the only book I'd brought along: the

The Champlain Boulevard now bites into the sheer face of Cape Diamond, where a plaque notes Montgomery's death.

"But the river is better than any silly old statue would be," said Tina. The St. Lawrence was especially impressive that day; its heavy ice was audibly rattling with the shift in a 15-foot tide. And certainly this rasping river dramatized the hardships these Americans overcame. They came incredibly close to capturing Canada, at least for a moment.

"Then the Canadians," said Kel, "might have fought their Revolution — against *us.*"

On a quiet Sunday afternoon, we tramped through the snow of Quebec Seminary, oldest boys' school in Canada and a spot where

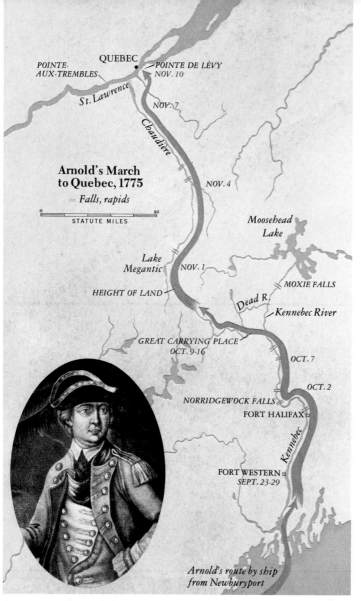

POINTE-
AUX-TREMBLES

QUEBEC

POINTE DE LÉVY
NOV. 10

St. Lawrence

NOV. 7

Chaudière

NOV. 4

**Arnold's March
to Quebec, 1775**

= *Falls, rapids*

0 _____ 50
STATUTE MILES

Moosehead
Lake

Lake
Megantic

NOV. 1

HEIGHT OF LAND

MOXIE FALLS

Dead R.

Kennebec River

GREAT CARRYING PLACE
OCT. 9-16

OCT. 7

OCT. 2

NORRIDGEWOCK FALLS

FORT HALIFAX

Kennebec

FORT WESTERN
SEPT. 23-29

*Arnold's route by ship
from Newburyport*

Benedict Arnold's march to invade Canada con-
quered uninhabited forest in one of the greatest
feats of the Americans' first aggressive campaign.
Arnold (oval inset) left Fort Western with 1,000
men, cramming supplies into clumsy batteaux
that often capsized when unskilled boatmen
poled them into rapids. Two soldiers' wives
shared and survived the hardships of the route,
winning the respect of all. Tired men carried the
heavy boats on their shoulders to bypass cascades
wilder than Maine's Moxie Falls (above). "A
direful howling wilderness not describable," one
soldier-diarist called this country. Among rough
hills, flooded valleys, and bewildering swamps,
the little force fought illness and starvation.
Only 600 arrived with Arnold to besiege Quebec.

journal kept by young Henry Dearborn, one
of the rebel prisoners. Suddenly the words
seemed to leap from the page:

"Hottel-dieu—which is a nunnery & Hospital. . . . Being indispos'd I got liberty to go
to the Hottel-dieu. . . . I remain'd . . . until . . .
I recovered my health. . . ."

When I saw Josh a few minutes later, I
read him the Dearborn passage. "It's the
same hospital," I told him.

"And I got my left leg hurt," said Josh,
"just like Colonel Arnold."

"Oh, no!" said Kel, horrified. "Josh is following in Benedict Arnold's footsteps!" Kel
had the advantage; he had already studied
history. But on the last day of 1775 Arnold

The McDowells scout the narrow streets of Quebec's Lower Town on New Year's Eve and take the measure of the cliff that splits the city. This cul-de-sac meets Rue Sault-au-Matelot, where Arnold went down with a bullet in his left leg.

On the bluff above Arnold's route, 19th-century cannon replace the guns that commanded the St. Lawrence River and its banks in December, 1775.

was still a hero, still a fine example for Josh to imitate.

From his own hospital bed in Lower Town on the last day of 1775, Arnold had written, "I am exceedingly apprehensive.... It is impossible to say what our future operations will be...."

The same sentiment was repeated by clear-headed Nathanael Greene at perhaps the same moment of the same day. He contemplated the enlistments that would lapse at midnight; in a few hours Washington's army around Boston would shrink by 2,000 men. "Nothing but confusion and disorder reign," wrote Greene. "...We never have been so weak as we shall be tomorrow."

And so the year 1776 arrived.

Rushing to meet Arnold's units for a surprise attack on New Year's Eve, Gen. Richard Montgomery reels backward mortally wounded, still holding his sword. In the snow-choked dark, his men falter before a barrier of sharpened logs. Both his assault and Colonel Arnold's failed.

Thomas Jefferson presents the Declaration of Independence to John Hancock, President of the Continenta

1776: "And Our Sacred Honor"

Congress. By adopting it, the delegates crowned their treason against the king and founded a new nation.

ON NEW YEAR'S DAY of 1776 the British regulars in Boston sighted a curious banner flying above the American lines on Prospect
Hill. Could this flag, they wondered, be a signal of surrender? George Washington was
amused when he heard the British reaction,
for "we had hoisted the union flag in compliment to the United Colonies."

Tina also wondered about that flag. "Was
it the one with 13 stars?" she asked. No, it
had 13 stripes and the crossed bars of the
Union Jack. Yet it marked "the day which gave
being to the new army," as Washington said.

Whole units had disappeared as enlistments lapsed, but Washington juggled his

companies, signed men up for one year's service, gambled on British inaction – and won.

Down the Atlantic coast, the year began
with fire and fury: "... at about quarter after
three o'clock, the British fleet lying off Norfolk, Virginia, commenced a cannonade ..."
read a newspaper report. "Regulars landed
and set fire to the town ... and the fire spread
with amazing rapidity."

Bitterness spread even faster. Men everywhere openly talked treason. In January a
new 81-page pamphlet appeared in Philadelphia, *Common Sense* by Thomas Paine: "Ye
that dare oppose not only the tyranny but the
tyrant, stand forth! ... Time hath found us!"

73

The people did stand forth—and increasingly they came to agree with Paine's famous call " 'TIS TIME TO PART." *Common Sense* was an instant, highly influential best seller.

"A few more of such flaming arguments, as were exhibited at Falmouth and Norfolk," wrote Washington in January, 1776, "added to the sound doctrine and unanswerable reasoning contained in the pamphlet '*Common Sense,*' will not leave numbers at a loss to decide upon the propriety of a separation."

If independence was in the air, so was war. On the very day that *Common Sense* went on sale in Philadelphia, George III concluded a contract with Duke Karl of Brunswick: German mercenaries would be leased—eventually about 30,000 of them. These "Hessians" would help Britain put down "the Rebellious Americans," as King George now called them. Using his quill to prod Lord Sandwich

and the navy, the king wrote, "we must shew that the English Lion . . . has added the swiftness of the Race Horse."

Not quite so swift—though surely surer—was young Henry Knox, our Little Ox, now inching toward Boston with 80 yokes of real oxen and a cargo on "42 exceeding strong sleds," as he called them. This was Fort Ticonderoga's "noble train of artillery," the cannon that Knox and his fellow Americans had dragged through winter snow and across frozen lakes. They would finally pull those cannon to the top of Dorchester Heights—and thus end the British occupation of Boston.

For the bitter moment, though, besieged Boston was suffering through its second winter of occupation. Only 3,500 civilians remained in the city. Fuel grew short. British regulars began to plunder empty houses and pull down fences. They had cut down the

Fog hides the highways from Lake Champlain to the Berkshires: Beyond the reconstructed stockade on Mount Defiance in New York, Henry Knox led a 42-sled ox train with 50-odd pieces of artillery from Fort Ticonderoga to Boston for Washington's siege of the British. Knox followed old Indian trails through deep snow. A "cruel thaw," as he termed it, thwarted him in January, 1776. Ice gave way, and cannon sank. He pulled them out, pushed on, and delivered them to a grateful general.

Liberty Tree out of spite, because patriots rallied there. It yielded 14 cords of firewood.

The siege of Boston illustrates a point true for most of the war: The British moved at will upon the sea while Americans moved on land with "the whole country, as it were, at their disposal," as General Howe explained to Lord George Germain. "Their armies retiring a few miles back from navigable rivers, ours cannot follow them...."

Nonetheless General Clinton had now set sail to poke along the coast. He would meet Sir Peter Parker's fleet with 3,000 troops who might attack anywhere in the South. Trying to counter him, Congress sent Gen. Charles Lee to dodge about the seaboard, as confused as "a dog in a dancing school," said Lee. The British could "fly in an instant to any spot where they chose with their canvass wings.... I can only act from surmise...."

The British had the initiative—but not enough troops to pacify all 13 colonies. How, then, did the British plan to win the war? With the help of colonials loyal to the king: "there are many inhabitants in every province well affected to Government, from whom no doubt we shall have assistance," General Howe wrote. But he hedged: The loyalists could not rally "until His Majesty's arms have a clear superiority by a decisive victory." The general needed a showdown battle.

But Boston was not the place for victory. After Fort Ti's big guns were trundled up to Dorchester Heights, Howe knew that his

stronghold was doomed. On the morning of March 17, Gen. John Sullivan examined the British defenses and "found all abandoned.... We then informed the General." So George Washington had a proper Irish messenger to deliver the St. Patrick's Day news: General Howe, his 7,000 troops, and his Tory friends had withdrawn from Boston.

Washington had won his first victory without fighting a battle—and just as well. As he wrote later, "... we should on all Occasions avoid a general Action, or put anything to the Risque, unless compelled by a necessity, into which we ought never to be drawn."

Just as the British banked on loyalists, so the patriots still hoped wistfully that the Canadians would rally to the cause. To review the situation, Congress sent a commission to Montreal, including Benjamin Franklin. The wise old printer was now a man of 70 years. But he set out in raw March weather to penetrate the American frontier more deeply than he had ever done before. He sailed up the Hudson, then changed to wagons, rowboats, and saddle horses, causing "a Fatigue that at my Time of Life may prove too much for me." Serenely, Franklin wrote a farewell letter to a friend—and went straight on to Montreal.

He found the city about as unfriendly to the occupying rebels as Boston had been to the British; the expedition could not be supplied by local sympathizers. If provisions were not sent, wrote Franklin, "the Army must starve, plunder, or surrender."

WATER COLOR BY FRANK T. MERRILL, JOHN HANCOCK MUTUAL LIFE INSURANCE COMPANY

General Howe, with sword drawn, personally directs the evacuation of British troops from Boston on March 17, 1776. American artillery dominates the city from Dorchester Heights, where Washington intently watches enemy movements. On the anniversary eve of the Boston Massacre—a date chosen by Washington to heighten morale—a work party of 1,200 men had moved by moonlight onto the hills of Dorchester peninsula with tools, carts, prefabricated breastworks, and the guns dragged from Fort Ticonderoga. Next morning, finished fortifications loomed above the British force, and the astonished Howe reported them the work of "12 or 14,000 Men."

ROWLAND SCHERMAN

Statue of William Pitt, great British statesman and long a popular hero among the colonists, still stands in Charleston, South Carolina, a monumental survivor of the 1776 attack. Four years later, a British cannon ball lopped off the right arm and hand that held the Magna Carta.

In Charleston harbor, Sir Peter Parker's nine-warship fleet pounds Fort Sullivan on June 28. Col. William Moultrie's ramparts, hastily built of spongy palmetto logs and sand, absorbed the shot. American artillery fired sparingly but to excellent effect; three of the hostile frigates ran aground. When British fire shattered the fort flagstaff, Sgt. William Jasper (left) defied the cannon to replace South Carolina colors.

General Howe took his forces in the same loyal direction to the foggy port of Halifax, Nova Scotia, to wait for supplies and reinforcements. But Washington knew full well Howe's eventual goal, New York, so he moved his headquarters there.

How did Washington know? New York's port was superb, loyalists were rife ("Internal, as well as external Enemies," said Washington), and the Hudson River cut New England off from the southern colonies. Incidentally, New York was a diverting city and Howe a man of the world.

No one knew when or where the masts of the Royal Navy would bristle onto the horizon. The colonials had to be ready everywhere. The king's loyal subjects were just as much in the dark. And so, in the thickets of North Carolina, the loyalists rallied too soon. In that part of the world, the king's friends were Scots: MacDonalds, Campbells, McLeods, McDowells. . .

"McDowells?" Josh said in great alarm. "We were on the wrong side?"

I tried to explain that many a family was divided in its loyalties. Benjamin Franklin's son William stood by the king—to his father's great distress. Henry Knox's wife Lucy was estranged from her Tory parents. "So McDowells fought on both sides, too," I told Josh. These Scots who had settled in the

Carolina sandhills had taken a special oath of loyalty to the king. In answer to the royal governor's call, they donned their kilts and rose royally to the skirl of bagpipes.

A thousand North Carolina patriots blocked the Scottish road to the coast. At a bridge on swampy Moores Creek, near the Cape Fear River, they manned earthworks. With skillful restraint, Col. James Moore lured the Scots into a trap.

"The battle lasted three minutes," a newspaper reported. Fifty Tories fell, and 850 trudged off as prisoners, among them Gen. Donald McDonald. Therewith, the spirit wheezed out of the Tory cause in North Carolina like bagpipes dropped to earth.

Josh wanted to know what happened to our own kinsmen. I couldn't tell him. Yet for the first time, I think, he realized what was meant by a civil war: The Battle of Moores Creek was fought entirely on both sides by men of the province. The blood and bitter-

ness spilled into that dank stream typifies much of the Revolutionary War in the South.

Moores Creek secured North Carolina for the patriots. But now General Clinton met Sir Peter Parker and sailed farther south. And finally at dawn one June morning Col. William Moultrie looked out beyond his defenses at Charleston, South Carolina: "... I saw a number of the enemy's boats in motion," he reported. "... I saw the men-of-war loose their topsails. I hurried back to the fort...." So began another decisive battle.

When Kel and I paced off the terrain on Sullivan's Island, he stopped to finger the palmetto logs displayed there. "It's spongy," he said. "They used *that* to build a fort?"

The palmetto was his only handy tree, and Colonel Moultrie used it well.

Gen. Charles Lee, when he arrived in Charleston, called the unfinished fort a "slaughter pen." By good luck, he was wrong. Clinton had already landed his troops nearby,

Sailing past the 200-foot steeple of Christ Church, a frigate plies the waters of Philadelphia's 2-mile-long harbor. With 40,000 people in 1775, visitors complained the city had a "thundering of Coaches, Chariots, Chaises, Waggons" off cobbled Elfreth's Alley, right.

CLYDE HARE

on the Isle of Palms; the ships forced their way past Moultrie in the narrow channel. "As soon as they came within the reach of our guns, we began to fire," wrote Colonel Moultrie. "They were soon abreast of the fort ... and begun their attack most furiously about 10 o'clock...." The palmetto logs, instead of splintering, simply swallowed the shot. And even today the flag of South Carolina flaunts a palmetto tree.

Kel and I stood near the spot where the defenders had manned their 26 cannon. We watched as a freighter entered the harbor, passing remarkably close to land.

"Moultrie's 18-pounders could easily cover half a mile," said James A. Turner, Jr., our guide around the island. Thus, Moultrie was able to defend the port.

Charles Lee had feared that British ships would come around to the west end of the fort where emplacements were still incomplete. And indeed, aboard his 50-gun flagship *Bristol,* Sir Peter Parker gave this order.

"But three of his ships ran aground on a sandbar there," said Jim Turner; on an old chart, he pointed to the obstruction called Lower Middle Ground. Two of the ships got free again, but the 28-gun frigate *Actaeon* remained hopelessly stranded.

Kel and I read the journal neatly penned

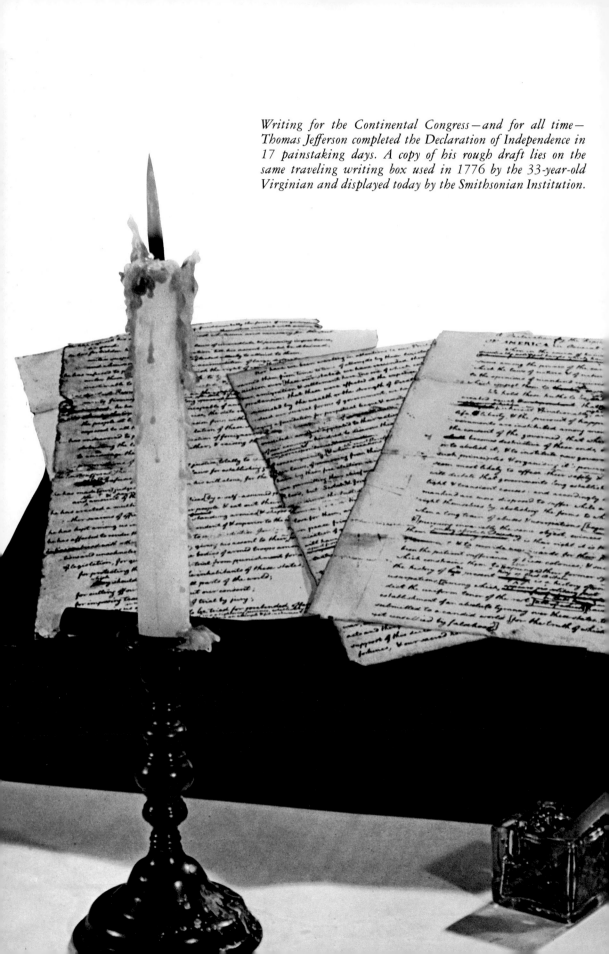

Writing for the Continental Congress—and for all time—Thomas Jefferson completed the Declaration of Independence in 17 painstaking days. A copy of his rough draft lies on the same traveling writing box used in 1776 by the 33-year-old Virginian and displayed today by the Smithsonian Institution.

Jefferson offers his work for the "judgments and amendments" of Franklin (left) and John Adams, who recalled, "we were all in haste; Congress was impatient."

by Maj. Barnard Elliott, an artillery officer on duty in Charleston. The British ships, he wrote, made "a Smart Cannonade, which was return'd with Coolness and deliberation from the Fort.... an incessant fire was kept up till Eleven O'Clock at Night." Then the Americans "had no more powder."

The British had suffered sharply; 64 had already died. The Americans sustained "but ten men ... killed & 22 wounded, so wonderfully did God appear in our behalf, that the Men of War cut their cables in the dead of Night & Stole away ..." wrote Major Elliott.

The victory bought two years of time free from British menace. Being southern, the defenders of Charleston also enjoyed moments of high drama. During the cannonade that Charles Lee called "the most furious fire I ever heard or saw," the fort's flagstaff was shattered. Sgt. William Jasper recklessly dashed out, restored the colors, and won his place in the folklore of the brave.

One American cannon ball brought trauma to Sir Peter Parker himself. As deserters told it, "the commodore had his breeches tore off, his backside laid bare."

83

"*Really?*" asked Kel. Sir Peter Parker's pants, celebrated in song and ballad, had the same gleeful effect on the patriots of 1776.

But for me, the stranded ship *Actaeon* and her sandbar made the most prophetic point. When the tide failed to float her, the British crew abandoned ship, leaving the *Actaeon* in flames. Fire turned the English oak to ash, and the last embers hissed and drowned on the treacherous shoal. Just how treacherous Kel and I saw as we surveyed Charleston Harbor; upon the same shoal later warriors built another fort that stands there yet, a bulky reminder that the *Actaeon's* fire would not be the last. Its name is Fort Sumter.

WHILE SOLDIERS were defending Sullivan's Island, other patriots were busy in Philadelphia at the Congress. Should they, at last, renounce all allegiance to Britain? Even Patrick Henry wondered about the timing of such a declaration. Weeks earlier, that advocate of independence John Adams had felt himself shunned like a man "with the Leprosy."

The oldest member of Congress, Benjamin Franklin, watched the British attitude harden, then felt the Congressional pulse on independence: "The Novelty ... deters some, the Doubt of Success, others, the vain Hope of Reconciliation, many. But our Enemies ... continually ... remove these Obstacles...."

At home, men were also changing their minds. The North Carolina Provincial Congress remembered the bagpipes on Moores Creek, learned of Clinton's expedition, and became the first with a clear statement: unanimously renouncing "the moderation hitherto manifested" and empowering their delegates to join "in declaring independency."

Now came June, "the busyest Month, that I ever saw," wrote John Adams to his wife.

Richard Henry Lee of Virginia presented a resolution: that the thirteen "United Colonies are, and of right ought to be, free and independent States...."

Delegates of six colonies voted against Lee's motion. Nevertheless, Congress named a five-man committee to prepare a declaration of independence — "that no time be lost."

This committee included Lee's fellow Virginian, the brilliant, 33-year-old Thomas Jefferson. Encouraged by his colleagues, he began the first draft alone in his rented rooms on Market Street. He showed his rough draft to John Adams and Franklin.

"We hold these truths to be sacred and undeniable...." Someone — perhaps Franklin — deleted the last three words and substituted "self-evident." Jefferson said foreign mercenaries were sent to "deluge us in blood." Franklin toned down the language; the Hessians would "destroy us." Jefferson accepted these changes for — as he explained years later — he wanted words "so plain and firm as to command ... assent."

While Jefferson improved his prose, Congress took up Lee's resolution. John Dickinson opposed it with passion. Robert Morris thought it premature. Yet, on July 2, the resolution of independence passed.

The date seemed important to Kel. "The Fourth of July is a fake!" said my teen-age iconoclast. "We should demand a recount!"

I had to admit that Kel stood in good company: "The Second Day of July 1776, will be

Floodlights stress the Georgian lines of Philadelphia's Independence Hall, etched in American history as the birthplace of independence and the Constitution. The silhouetted statue honors Commodore John Barry, naval hero of the Revolution. In the first-floor doorway, the Liberty Bell fascinates young visitors; it cracked in 1835 tolling in mourning at the death of John Marshall, Continental soldier and later Chief Justice of the United States.

N.G.S. PHOTOGRAPHERS JAMES L. STANFIELD (LEFT) AND B. ANTHONY STEWART

King George crashes down in New York City on the night of July 9, after Washington's announcement of independence to his troops. The gilded lead statue, erected in 1770 on the Bowling Green, showed His Majesty crowned and mounted on horseback but lacking stirrups — proper equipment for a tyrant, said wags, "to ride a hard-trotting horse." The mob pulled down the statue, broke it up, and sent most of the pieces to Connecticut where munitions makers turned them into 42,000 bullets.

DRAWING BY EDWIN AUSTIN ABBEY

Striking a blow for liberty after hearing the Declaration of Independence for the first time, citizens in Philadelphia knock down the Royal Arms and burn them in the street. When Rhode Island legislators in Newport learned of the Declaration, they sent out for a punchbowl — traditionally the 12-inch earthenware vessel at right called the Liberty Bowl. From it, they toasted independence.

First printed report on independence appears in Philadelphia's Pennsylvanischer Staatsbote *on July 5: "Yesterday the Honorable Congress ... declared the United Colonies Free and Independent States."*

ral-Adjudant) und Capitain Burr, welche zu Quebec zu gefangenen gemacht wurden als der würdigste General Montgomery daselbst ein opfer der Ministerialischen rache wurde, jetzt an bord der Ministerialischen flotte zu Sandy-Hook sind.

Die rede gehet durchgängig, daß unsere kreuzfahrer 30 transportschiffe gegen Osten zu genommen haben.

Philadelphia, den 5 July.

Gestern hat der Achtbare Congreß dieses Vesten Landes die Vereinigten Colonien Freye und Unabhängige Staaten erkläret.

Die Declaration in Englisch ist jetzt in der Presse; sie ist datirt, den 4ten July, 1776, und wird heut oder morgen im druck erscheinen.

the most memorable Epocha, in the History of America," wrote no less a witness than John Adams. "It ought to be commemorated, as the Day of Deliverance.... It ought to be solemnized with Pomp and Parade, with Shews, Games, Sports, Guns, Bells, Bonfires and Illuminations from one End of this Continent to the other from this Time forward forever more."

So, on the advice of Kel and John Adams, our family celebrated the Glorious Second of July by visiting Philadelphia's Independence Hall; we dropped by again on the Fourth. During those visits, we got the feel of time and place. Through the great windows of the Assembly Room, we could catch glimpses—as delegates did in '76—of the

Swimming for their lives, Americans retreat across Gowanus Creek during the Battle of Long Island, with the 1st Maryland Regiment bravely covering the withdrawal. Below, modern Marylanders re-enact the musket work. Approaching New York in July, General Howe established a base on Staten Island, then landed 20,000 troops on Long Island. He outflanked Washington with a night march, defeated him roundly, and forced him back northward with his weakened army.

ENGRAVING BY JAMES SMILLIE AFTER PAINTING BY ALONZO CHAPPEL, FROM "BATTLES OF THE UNITED STATES" BY HENRY E. DAWSON

TERRILL E. EILER

American and British
forces continue to
White Plains

Pell's
Point

FORT LEE □ □ FORT WASHINGTON

Throg's Neck

✕ HARLEM HEIGHTS

Hudson

Kip's Bay

NEWARK •

MANHATTAN
ISLAND

NEW
YORK •

LONG
ISLAND

East River

Gowanus
Creek

✕ BROOKLYN HEIGHTS

STATEN
ISLAND

American forces in blue
British forces in red

ATLANTIC OCEAN

0   10
STATUTE MILES

COLOR ENGRAVING BY FRANCOIS XAV. HABERMANN, LIBRARY OF CONGRESS

adjoining square with full-leafed summery trees. The Assembly Room actually seemed larger now than I had remembered. The State House in Boston and the Capitol in Williamsburg had no room so tall and grand.

In 1776, men bitterly, noisily raised their voices here. Delegates quarreled over Jefferson's phrases, deleting some. The frecklefaced Virginian sat next to Dr. Franklin, "who perceived that I was not insensible to these mutilations," Jefferson later remembered.

"I have made it a rule," Franklin confided to his young friend, "...to avoid becoming the draftsman of papers to be reviewed by a public body."

At last, on July 4, Congress adopted Jefferson's revised Declaration of Independence.

"But that old Trumbull painting doesn't show them signing," said Kel. Delegates waited for an engrossed copy. On July 8, outside the Hall, the Declaration was read to a crowd of Philadelphians. On August 2, most of the members of Congress signed it—but not all: At least one signed as late as November. And all of the 56 signatures but President John Hancock's and Secretary Charles Thomson's were kept secret until 1777.

"Were they really afraid?" asked Tina, who had always assumed the Founding Fathers were fearless. The last words of the Declaration itself answered her question: "...we mutually pledge to each other our Lives, our Fortunes and our sacred Honor."

Together they had committed an act of treason. They knew the risks—death by hanging for themselves, poverty and dishonor for their families—and still they signed. Secrecy was the minimum prudence.

They made nervous jokes of gallows humor. Heavy Benjamin Harrison chuckled; when his turn came at the British noose, he said, his weight would bring him swift mercy.

Windswept fire rages through British-held New York, charring 493 buildings, during the night of September 20. The uneasy British—and even many Americans—blamed patriot arsonists, like the one below, but historians believe the fire started accidentally. The redcoats rounded up suspects by the score, some at bayonet-point.

FROM "CASSELL'S HISTORY OF THE UNITED STATES" BY EDMUND OLLIER

But the risk was real. Of the 56 signers, 15 had their homes destroyed in the war. Some signers were seized by the British and thrown in jail. Others narrowly missed capture; and still others experienced the heartbreak of seeing their libraries burned, their colts killed, their children taunted as sons of traitors.

"Their *colts* killed?" my daughter asked in shock. It was true. When British soldiers raided Jefferson's farm, they seized all horses big enough to travel—and cut the throats of the foals they left behind. Tina regarded this act as a major atrocity.

Many an American recoiled from the Declaration. Washington's friend Bryan Fairfax sided with his king. John Dickinson, who refused to sign the Declaration, was still willing to fight beside his neighbors.

But the street crowd showed no such brainy restraint. Everywhere, until the last frontier settlement got the news in September, communities were busy with their celebrations.

Typical was Worcester, Massachusetts, where thirsty patriots "repaired to the tavern, lately known by the sign ... King's Arms," reported Isaiah Thomas's newspaper. The royal sign was removed and toasts were offered for "Prosperity and perpetuity to the United States of America" and about two dozen other noble things—including one toast to "Perpetual itching without the benefit of scratching to the enemies of America."

When she heard that one, Tina rolled in mirth—then halted abruptly and counted the toasts. "They had thirteen drinks before that one," she said. "Do you think they were—*drunk?*" But I read on: "The greatest decency and good order was observed...."

On the evening of July 9, at George Washington's order, the Declaration of Independence was read to all the troops in New York to provide "fresh incentive ... to act with

Fidelity and Courage," for a free country.

Just a week earlier an observer had looked seaward and noticed "something resembling a wood of pine trees trimmed....in about ten minutes, the whole Bay was full of shipping....I thought all London was afloat." By afternoon, more than 100 British ships had anchored off Sandy Hook. The battle for Long Island would soon begin.

Washington had no more than 10,000 men to guard a 15-mile front on Long Island. Neither he nor his soldiers had ever faced the British for a pitched battle in the open field. General Howe landed some 9,000 able-bodied "experienced Veterans," as Washington

described them, on Staten Island. Worst of all, the bays, inlets, sounds, and rivers around New York permitted the Royal Navy to land troops at will. Soon Clinton returned with his 3,000. Crack Hessians came from Germany, until Howe had about 30,000 troops. And, to command his squadron, in sailed Richard, Admiral Viscount Howe himself, swarthy "Black Dick."

General Washington prepared for the battle with energy—collecting militia, building fortifications, sinking hulks offshore, installing batteries to close the rivers. But he ignored one cardinal rule of warfare: He divided his army in the face of a superior enemy. Nearly

Nathan Hale, arrested and condemned to hang as a self-confessed American spy, calmly awaits execution in New York. General Howe, fearing an attack on the burned city, gave the order carried out by William Cunningham, his brutal provost marshal. An eyewitness wrote that Hale "behaved with great composure" when he said, "I only regret that I have but one life to lose for my country."

It didn't come. The general wanted help from his admiral brother; but the ships could not enter the East River against a northeast wind. Instead of retreating back across the East River, Washington actually reinforced his foothold on Brooklyn Heights — two square miles around a Brooklyn ferry.

Complete American defeat seemed only a matter of time as General Howe began to raise siege works. But rain moved in from the northeast, drenching troops in their barricades — and still holding back the British ships from the East River.

Thus George Washington — a green general humble enough to learn — had time to reconsider: He chose to evacuate Long Island in the dark of night. The Americans had only ten flat-bottomed boats on hand. But on Washington's orders, they found more — ostensibly to bring more men, since success of the retreat completely depended on secrecy.

And who could manage this fantastic ferry service? Washington turned to authentic mariners from Massachusetts: John Glover's Marbleheaders and Israel Hutchinson's men from Salem, Lynn, and Danvers — fishermen, sailors, dockside tradesmen who knew the temper of tides and wind.

At 10 p.m., Gen. Alexander McDougall, himself a mariner-merchant, ordered the first unit to embark. With neither light nor noise, the ferries moved back and forth that night between Brooklyn and Manhattan. At midnight, the wind changed and an ebbing tide threatened the retreat with disaster. Sloops and other sailing craft were halted and Glover had too few rowboats to do the job in one night. Any men left behind would be doomed.

Then, miraculously, the wind shifted once more. Sails filled. Some 9,000 men were moved that night — with their guns and matériel. And after dawn, as the last of the army sailed away, one young captain noted that the boats now moved under "the friendly cover of a thick fog."

With enormous luck and a choir of skills,

half his force stayed on Manhattan; perhaps 10,000 guarded Long Island, and especially the strategic Brooklyn Heights.

At 9 a.m. on August 27, the Americans heard the signal of British cannon — but on the American rear. By a brilliant night march, Henry Clinton had slipped around to the east, had outflanked Generals Sullivan and Stirling. Soon both of them and some 800 other Americans were prisoners, for the surprise had been complete.

At his Brooklyn earthworks, Washington himself rallied the fugitives. "Remember what you are contending for!" he shouted. They waited for General Howe's assault.

Washington and his mariners had saved the new nation's army: "and to our great Astonishment," admitted a British officer next day. Washington wrote frankly to Congress about his men's "apprehension and despair."

But John Adams best analyzed the Battle of Long Island: "In general, our Generals were outgeneralled...."

For two weeks, the British paused while

British men-of-war force a passage up the Hudson through smoke billowing from the guns of Fort Lee, high on the New Jersey Palisades, and Fort Washington on the New York bank. American fire and obstructions proved ineffective. Finally the British took Fort Washington and 2,818 prisoners. Washington watched from Fort Lee (left), which he lost to the redcoats only four days later.

Admiral Lord Howe tried to negotiate peace with the Americans. Benjamin Franklin saw little hope; as he wrote Lord Howe, "... were it possible for *us* to forget and forgive ... it is not possible for *you* ... to forgive the People you have so heavily injured." Britain must first recognize American independence. But "I know too well her abounding Pride and deficient Wisdom, to believe she will ever take such salutary Measures."

Still, Franklin joined John Adams and Edward Rutledge for a meeting with Lord Howe on Staten Island. On the way, Franklin and Adams had to share the same room and even the same bed. They argued briefly over whether to keep the only window open or shut. Franklin and fresh air won.

That was the only victory of the conference. As Lord Howe's secretary Ambrose

Serle said, "They met, they talked, they parted. And now, nothing remains but to fight it out...."

The fight for New York had already been settled with the loss of Long Island. But for political reasons, the second largest city had to be defended. "I could wish to maintain it," Washington wrote Congress, but he knew even the attempt might be "most fatal."

American desertions rose; in a few days' time, 13 Connecticut militia units melted from 8,000 to 2,000 men. Washington did his best to reorganize his forces.

Then on the sunny Sunday, September 15, British warships moved into the East River and pounded Kip's Bay. General Howe landed his troops and found no opposition. The bombardment had erased the American earthworks—and the defenders had fled. "The demons of fear and disorder seemed to take full possession..." one American private said.

"Take the walls!" roared General Washington, astride his horse. "Take the cornfield!" A few soldiers responded, but the panic was almost complete. "I used every means in my power, to...get them into some order," Washington recalled, "but my attempts were fruitless." Suddenly, about 60 British soldiers appeared; Washington and his aides were left to face them without so much as a musket, to escape at a gallop, furious and humiliated.

Kip's Bay cost the British three dead and some 18 wounded. With those casualties, they purchased New York.

On the night of September 20, patriot

Freshwater fleet to defend Lake Champlain—a strategic route between the rebel colonies and Canada—grows amid the forest at Skenesborough, New York. Benedict Arnold directed construction (above) of 17 armed craft in the summer of 1776. The British, moving from Canada, had to stop to build their own 53-vessel flotilla.

96

sentries on the bluffs of Harlem Heights saw the New York sky redden angrily. One-fourth of the city burned that night and next day. The scene was wild. General Howe, fearing an American trick and attack, refused at first to spare his troops to fight the flames. The Britons blamed the Yankees. And even Washington suspected that perhaps "some good honest fellow" had set the fire to deny the British winter quarters.

Whatever the cause, the ashes were still hot when the British seized a heavily muscled young man named Nathan Hale, a Connect-icut captain wearing civilian clothes within British lines. He had volunteered for this intelligence mission.

"I wish to be useful," he had explained, "and every kind of service, necessary to the public good, becomes honorable by being necessary." And so, this young man—a schol-ar, an athlete, a patriot, and now a secret agent—took his Yale College diploma into New York City to pose as a schoolmaster. Possibly he was betrayed by a Tory relative.

However it happened, General Howe him-self—worried over American fires and plots—ordered Nathan Hale hanged as a self-con-fessed spy on Sunday, September 22. A com-passionate British captain reported that Hale, waiting near the gallows, "was calm, and bore himself with gentle dignity, in the conscious-ness of rectitude and high intentions," with his closing words: "I only regret that I have but one life to lose for my country."

If these words sound like a quotation from Addison, who really cares? Captain Hale,

Sole relic of the October, 1776, fighting on Lake Champlain —when Gen. Guy Carleton's fleet overwhelmed Arnold's —the Philadelphia *now levels her bow gun at visitors to the Smithsonian Institution in Washington. A 24-pound cannon ball smashed her hull; engineers raised her in 1935.*

Retreating across New Jersey through cold, rain, and mud, Washington leads 4,000 troops in the bitter withdrawal of 1776. A "melancholy situation," he wrote. "Our little handful is daily decreasing." In three months he had lost 5,000 men captured by the British. Fearing to lose the city of Philadelphia next, Washington found "the Spirits of the People . . . quite sunk."

age 21, did not claim to be first with his phrase, nor first to die for his country.

He was assuredly not the last patriot to be seized by the nervous British. On the same Sunday, they arrested a young Jew from Poland, one Haym Salomon. They threw him into jail. According to tradition, they later moved him to the Provost, New York's most infamous prison. There, as time passed, Salomon's health would weaken while his resolution grew stronger.

It was mid-October before General Howe moved in force again. But when he did, his moves were relentless. The brothers Howe played an amphibious game of leapfrog at Throg's Neck and Pell's Point. Washington moved north to White Plains; then, with another engagement, he fell back behind the Croton River. Now Howe took Fort Washington and all its stores; almost 3,000 Americans fell prisoner — and the very name Washington lost luster.

There was no time to dress the wound; a few days later the British crossed the Hudson to surprise Fort Lee. Gen. Nathanael Greene and his garrison barely escaped; their precious cannon and supplies — even a thousand barrels of flour — were left behind.

So, in the rain of late November, the Americans began their dark ordeal of retreat across New Jersey.

Virtually all the news was bad: On Lake Champlain, Guy Carleton had brushed aside Benedict Arnold's makeshift fleet — and now Carleton could move on Fort Ticonderoga at his leisure. . . . Gen. Charles Lee was taken prisoner, to the despair of all who thought him a genius . . . Congress, meeting in a threatened Philadelphia, grew restive, then moved to Baltimore.

Followed closely by the redcoats, sometimes in sight of them, Washington ran his necessary, disgraceful race: The army had to be saved at all costs, and "if overpowered," Washington was quoted as saying in Newark,

"we must cross the Allegheny Mountains."

In the same city, one volunteer used a drum as his desk and with cold fingers began slowly shaping some forceful words about the summer soldier and the sunshine patriot. Tom Paine had begun his *Crisis* papers.

On the last day of November, 2,060 enlistments expired. The men went home. Others waited only until their service would end on New Year's Eve. But many would refuse to wait. Desertions increased sharply. Without fresh troops for 1777, Washington confided to his brother John Augustine, *"I think the game is pretty near up."*

So his boats ferried the little army into

PAINTING BY HOWARD PYLE, WILMINGTON SOCIETY OF THE FINE ARTS, DELAWARE ART CENTER

Pennsylvania; the Delaware River would offer protection. At least until it froze solid enough for marching troops.

Then, in America's darkest hour, General Howe followed military custom and settled down in winter quarters. He would let the Hessians guard that outpost at Trenton.

For Howe, the year 1776 was ending quietly and victoriously. Soon, the war itself might be finished. In New Jersey, loyal subjects were flocking to swear King George allegiance. New York seemed a friendly city.

But George Washington "never appeared to full advantage but in difficulties and in action," observed the keen Tom Paine.

Washington himself listed some of his most pressing difficulties in a hasty letter to Robert Morris:

"...by the first of next Month then, we shall...fall short of, 1200 men....for you may as well attempt to stop the Winds from blowing...as the Regiments from going when their term is expired." Yet before his troops vanished, he had plans for "the poor remains of our debilitated Army."

The campaign of 1776 had ended for the British and Hessians. But for that dangerous Virginia farmer and his cold men, the campaign of 1777 would start early—with a Christmas feast.

Ice-clogged Delaware River hampers Washington's army in Emanuel Leutze's idealized painting. The bol

1777: "Times That Try Men's Souls"

attack at Trenton, on December 26, 1776, surprised the Hessians and gave America her first great victory.

OF ALL OUR TRIPS to battlefields and historic sites, our Delaware crossing stands alone. We drove through a blizzard to get there.

"Is the wind northeast?" asked Josh. Washington's had been a northeast wind, so the youngsters were glad to see snow sticking to the proper side of tree trunks. A Bucks County historian assured us that she had never before seen weather so closely imitate the storms reported at Christmastime, 1776. On the Delaware River itself, a strong current moved whole flotillas of ice floes—chunks thick enough to be a hazard to boats.

An annual re-enactment of the famous crossing was scheduled for December 26, but we wanted to be purists. So we arrived early, checked into a motel on Christmas Eve, then foraged tediously for an open restaurant on Christmas morning. Josh, our natural dramatist, felt we were "hungry just like Washington's men." Still, we visited the banks of the Delaware on the anniversary of its great event.

A highway bridge now straddles the river, but the stone house of McKonkey's ferry still stands. I parked the car nearby and let the children romp through the snowdrifts.

Christmas lights deck a bridge at Washington Crossing; ice paves the Pennsylvania side of the Delaware, trapping a 40-foot copy of the ore boats patriots used almost two centuries ago.

When they returned to thaw out, I read to them from some of the books we had brought.

"These are the times that try men's souls. The Summer soldier and the sunshine Patriot will, in this crisis, shrink from the service of their country; but he that stands it *now*, deserves the love and thanks of man and woman ... the harder the conflict the more glorious the triumph...."

Those words from Paine's *The Crisis* were published December 19, 1776, in the *Pennsylvania Journal.* Washington got a copy just in time. He ordered the papers read to each corporal's squad. Those were the words, written on a drumhead during a gloomy retreat, that now inspired men to turn and attack.

My children paid Tom Paine their ultimate tribute: total silence. The American army must have had the same reaction, for these words demand the quiet clenching of a fist.

Later that same Christmas evening we tucked Rob away, and the older children joined me again on the Pennsylvania bank of the Delaware. There I read them an account attributed to one of Washington's aides.

"*Dec. 25* — Christmas morning. They make a great deal of Christmas in Germany, and no doubt the Hessians will drink ... beer and have a dance tonight. They will be sleepy tomorrow morning. Washington will set the tune for them about daybreak....

"*Christmas, 6 P.M.* — The regiments have had their evening parade, but ... are marching toward the ferry. It is fearfully cold and raw and a snowstorm setting in.... It will be a terrible night for the soldiers who have no

Holiday callers, the McDowells visit the home where generals conferred on plans for Trenton.

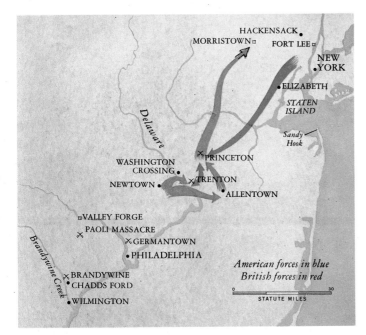

At the Delaware, an army turned around. With it, turned a war and American history. After the fall of Fort Lee and the New Jersey retreat, Washington took cover in Newtown, Pennsylvania, on December 8. He returned to take Trenton on December 26, then went back to Pennsylvania. He recrossed the river, marched to Allentown, and took Princeton on January 3, 1777, then Hackensack and Elizabeth three days later. Now the army could rest safely at Morristown.

103

Americans encircle and capture Trenton. Here, red standards distinguish them and green banners mark the Hessians. Before Washington's command post, Henry Knox's battery (A) rakes the streets as Alexander Hamilton brings up his guns (B). To the west, Hugh Mercer's men take a flank position (C). In sight of the Delaware, John Sullivan's column (D) swings around the river road, south of the village, to secure the bridge (E) over Assunpink Creek, where some of the enemy escaped. Startled Hessians form and await orders by St. Michael's Church (F); their guns (G) duel briefly with Knox's. Driven from the town by musket and cannon, Col. Johann Rall tries to break out eastward past the Friends' Meeting House (H); Sullivan's force (I) turns him back and other patriot units block the way northward. Rall attempts to retake the town but falls wounded; his men regroup near the orchard (J). Repulsed in a last sally (K), the leaderless Germans surrender.

PAINTED FOR NATIONAL GEOGRAPHIC BY RICHARD SCHLECHT

shoes. Some of them have tied old rags around their feet. . . ."

Josh interrupted to ask, "What time is it right now?" It was close to 5:30, but our clearing western sky gave us more twilight than Washington's troops had seen. We watched shadows streak the riverbanks and turn the water to ink. Now firmly frozen in the ice was a 40-foot-long reproduction of a Durham ore boat. We could see how John Glover's Marblehead sailormen, with a flotilla of such craft, could transport a cargo of 2,400 soldiers, Henry Knox's 18 fieldpieces, and some horses.

Our riverscape darkened, and I turned on my flashlight to read further:

"*Dec. 26, 3 A.M. . . .*" The troops are all over, and the boats have gone back for the artillery. . . . I never have seen Washington so deter-mined as he is now. He stands on the bank of the river, wrapped in his cloak, superintend-ing the landing of his troops. He is calm and collected, but very determined. . . ."

On this one military exploit Washington was risking half of his crumbling army, all of his hope, and the undetermined future of the United States of America.

He had planned the Battle of Trenton as a three-pronged attack. But his men down-stream couldn't cross the river. Washington's own column was the only one that reached the New Jersey shore ready to march those nine miles to Trenton—and to fight. Wash-ington himself was late—too late, he feared in the dawn light, to surprise the Hessians. But Germanic feasting made the difference. The commander, Col. Johann Gottlieb Rall, had enjoyed his wine and cards through all

of Christmas night. He had just begun to sleep off his party when American troops simultaneously entered both ends of town.

A Hessian lieutenant roused Rall, who threw on his clothes, mounted his horse, and tried desperately to organize a defense. But Knox's cannon raked the streets, and American infantry cut off escape from the village. Rall ordered a bayonet charge, with his proud German band making brassy music to urge the men on. Then muskets and rifles began to blast from windows along the streets. The Americans had dried their wet flints in the warmth of Trenton homes. They took deadly aim; Rall toppled from his horse, mortally wounded. His men soon surrendered.

By 9:30 a.m. the day's fighting was done. Not one American had been killed. Only 500 Hessians escaped. Washington took nearly 1,000 prisoners, six brass fieldpieces, 40 horses, 1,000 muskets and rifles, musical instruments, and 40 barrels of rum. The latter presented a danger, so Washington ordered all the casks staved in to prevent what his troops called "Barrel Fever."

Washington had hoped to press on, but his small force now had prisoners and booty to tend. The storm still raged, so Washington again crossed the Delaware — westward to Pennsylvania for rest and new preparations. He could move again, he calculated, on December 29. But just two days after that, his enlisted men would leave. The opportunity was great — and fleeting. There was only one thing to do: Washington must make a personal appeal to the men. He had always avoided oratory; now he had to move men to risk their lives. He would even pledge his own credit against the bonus he offered soldiers who would stay another six weeks.

The troops gathered and General Washington spoke as well as he could. Would volunteers step forward? An awkward and terrible moment followed. *Not a single man stepped out.* The general simply tried again, returning to repeat his arguments. Something in his second appeal struck the hearts of those cold, battlesick men. A few came forward, then more. Then almost all.

Now the move against Princeton was possible. In a way, it was the most daring gamble of all, since the British were now alert — and led by a tough, swift officer, Charles, second Earl Cornwallis. The last day of 1776, in fact, was Cornwallis's thirty-eighth birthday. And that was the very day that Washington and 5,200 men, about half of them militia, completed another crossing of the Delaware and grouped themselves in Trenton.

Cornwallis and 8,000 crack regulars were on their way to meet the threat, and perhaps to destroy Washington completely. Rain and muddy roads slowed the British, but by the evening of January 2 they seemed to have pinned the Americans into a hopeless spot: retreat cut off by the Delaware. The night

PAINTING BY ALONZO CHAPPEL, CHICAGO HISTORICAL SOCIETY

Mortally wounded, Col. Johann Rall, commander of the Hessian forces at Trenton, surrenders his sword to Washington in this romanticized painting. Called "noisy . . . and a drunkard" by a British soldier, Rall had spent Christmas drinking and playing cards, despite warnings of an attack.

grew bitter and both armies lighted camp-fires. Chilled British sentries could hear American shovels working through the night.

Next morning the British discovered a hoax: A party of 500 Americans had burned fence-rails all night and noisily scraped with spades. Washington's whole army had slipped away on hard-frozen ground: not slinking westward in retreat—but boldly taking the offensive! They had moved around Corn-wallis's flank, and now surprised British reinforcements at Princeton. The tightly stretched British line of outposts snapped. American contingents took Hackensack and Elizabeth: Howe had to fall back. In 11 astonishing days, Washington liberated almost all of New Jersey.

But strategic as New Jersey was, the greatest value lay in American morale. We can even view the dramatic change through Ambrose Serle's British spectacles. On Christmas Eve, his diary clucked at a Congressional declaration as "the dying Groans of Rebellion." But the day after Trenton, "I was exceedingly concerned...as it will tend to revive the drooping Spirits of the Rebels and increase their Force...."

Serle was right.

Superstitious folk had feared the coming of 1777, for the numerals resembled a gallows: Rebels would hang that year. But suddenly the gallows seemed remote.

Congress even felt emboldened to publish the names of the men who had signed the Declaration of Independence. By crossing the Delaware, Washington convinced Americans that they could win the war. The war itself had turned.

But if Trenton and Princeton had convinced Americans, the news had not yet reached or convinced the royal courts on the other side of the Atlantic. It was my wife

Princeton University's venerable Nassau Hall, built in 1756, served as barracks and hospital for both British and American troops. A wall still shows scars gouged by cannonballs from Alexander Hamilton's battery during the Battle of Princeton on January 3. One shot, legend says, decapitated a portrait of George II. Not far from the building, British troops bayoneted Gen. Hugh Mercer (right), to the outrage of Americans. George Washington Parke Custis, Washington's adopted stepgrandson, painted the battle scene.

Martha who found a New Year's story from King George's palace. The account came from the Baroness Frederika von Riedesel, wife of the Brunswick general whom George III had hired for American fighting. The general had already gone to Canada; his baroness was in London, preparing to follow him off to war—and to take their three daughters with her. For New Year's Day, 1777, the baroness was invited to the Court of St. James's.

"I found the palace very ugly and furnished in an old-fashioned style," she wrote. The king chatted confidently about America.

The queen was also friendly and discussed the coming trip. "I admire your courage," she told the baroness, "for that is a great undertaking, and especially difficult with three children." My wife, who had been traveling with four children herself, felt the baroness a true heroine and Queen Charlotte a sage.

Across the English Channel, the new year 1777 had brought the French fad of Franklin-watching. The old philosopher had ignored the British navy to sail for Europe, and had arrived in Paris just before Christmas.

"Figure me in your Mind," he wrote a friend, "as jolly as formerly...very plainly dressed, wearing my thin grey straight Hair...under...a fine fur Cap, which comes down to my Forehead almost to my Spectacles. Think how this must appear among the powdered Heads of Paris." Shrewdly, Franklin

played the role of Noble Rustic, even wearing his plain brown coat to the dazzling court of Versailles when the king finally granted him an audience. He came, of course, as a well-established celebrity, the captor of electricity and the inventor of almost everything. Even Queen Marie Antoinette had taken lessons to play on the tuned-glass instrument that Franklin had invented and called the "armonica." Now she insisted that Dr. Franklin stand beside her at a palace party while she gambled for high stakes.

Franklin's own gamble in France was greater. The young U.S.A. desperately needed money, supplies—and, if possible, fighting allies. The French court was already helping secretly. His Most Christian Majesty Louis XVI, just 22 and not yet three years on the throne, preferred tinkering with locks to running his kingdom. But the foreign minister, Vergennes, ably handled matters.

Working with the Bourbons of Spain, Vergennes had set up a dummy firm with cash, credit, and high-quality gunpowder for the American patriots. He wanted to go to war openly, but his cautious fellow ministers and Louis XVI held him back.

Franklin meantime did what he could. Washington needed engineers, map-makers, and others skilled in military arts. Franklin's colleague Silas Deane had already signed contracts with more than a dozen French officers including the extraordinary, talented, and rich 19-year-old Marquis de Lafayette, who bought a ship to carry himself, the Baron de Kalb, and other adventurers to South Carolina. Franklin wrote Washington, urging him to protect "that amiable young Nobleman" from his "extreme Generosity."

EUROPEAN OFFICERS began to write a variety of records in America. That gallant Polish engineer, Tadeusz Kosciuszko, had already arrived in America at his own expense. The Polish patriot Casimir Pulaski needed a letter from Franklin and ship fare from Deane. A young French artist, Pierre Charles L'Enfant, had convinced Deane that he could make useful sketches or maps; so he now joined the parade crossing the Atlantic.

Lesser talents also heard the call, until volunteers became Franklin's "perpetual Torment." Yet, intuitive judge of men that he was, Franklin took note of one unemployed captain and personally promoted him:

Frederick William Augustus von Steuben, "lately a Lieutenant General in the king of Prussia's Service," Franklin wrote home in exaggerated introduction. The sage had guessed right: Congress had had trouble with some foreign officers—but there was always room for a German of such high credentials.

By summer, General Howe observed "the increased powers...of the enemy...their officers being much better...."

The British were now preparing an elaborate operation, worthy of dramatist Burgoyne himself. Handsome Jack would lead a mighty army from Canada down Lake Champlain and the Hudson River to Albany. From Fort Oswego, Lt. Col. Barry St. Leger would proceed down the Mohawk River to meet him. The garrison at New York would stage a diversion to help him, and Howe would give him orders for the next act.

If the British held the Hudson, they could cut the rebel states in two.

But Howe had obtained a license from London for a production in another theater.

Burgoyne raised his curtain on June 13 at the harbor of St. Johns on the forested Richelieu River. An embroidered flag—the royal standard, replete with lions—was run up and all the vessels of a river fleet fired a salute. Burgoyne had his overture.

The very next day in Philadelphia another flag made news in far quieter fashion: The Congress adopted a 13-star flag ("representing a new constellation") as the standard of the U.S.A.; in time it would change and age into Old Glory. But this small irony Burgoyne naturally missed. He was off, wrapped in a manifesto, to save the "suffering Thousands" from "unnatural Rebellion."

With him he had 3,700 British troops, General von Riedesel's 3,000 Germans (many of them limping through forests in the thigh-high cavalry jackboots), and 400 Indians, whom Burgoyne had firmly lectured against unnecessary bloodshed.

In July, Burgoyne took Fort Ti without a fight, simply by moving guns up neglected Mount Sugar Loaf and rendering the fort untenable. "The King, on receiving the account

Massive Greek portico in Princeton Battlefield Memorial Park honors unknown American and British dead. Designed by Thomas U. Walter, architect of the U.S. Capitol dome, it stands in a circle of pines enclosing the common grave.

of taking Ticonderoga," Horace Walpole told it, "ran into the Queen's room, crying, 'I have beat them! beat all the Americans!'"

His Majesty erred. As Burgoyne pushed on toward the Hudson River valley, he found the going hard. The Americans had carried away all food supplies, felled trees across the trails, smashed bridges, dammed creeks to make new swamps. Burgoyne, loaded down with his cargo of war, picked his way sweatily —20 miles in 20 days—as summer wasted away. August was half gone.

Modern highways now lace this big, partly forested country—roads so smooth that on a Sunday morning we drove right past the house we wanted in Fort Edward.

"There!" shouted Josh. "Stop! It's Jane McCrea's place."

Jane McCrea was a Presbyterian preacher's daughter who was planning to marry a Tory with Burgoyne's army. Jane had come to Fort Edward to meet her sweetheart, but instead she encountered the barbarity of Burgoyne's Indians. ("And that's the house where they grabbed her," said Josh.) According to the widely repeated story, Jane was shot, then scalped. Accurate or not, this report enraged America and shocked Europe: Savages had been loosed upon the innocent.

There was surely substance to the charge in the Mohawk valley; St. Leger's British forces included 875 white men—and substantially more Indian allies. They defeated Nicholas Herkimer at Oriskany, but patriots checked them at Fort Stanwix.

Then Benedict Arnold used the cleverest

On Brandywine Creek, willows weep where patriots bled.
In the late summer of 1777, at Head of Elk, Maryland,
General Howe landed 16,000 troops for a move on Philadelphia, 45 miles northeast. Hoping to block him, Washington deployed 11,000 troops along the Brandywine,
among them the French nobleman and new major general,
the Marquis de Lafayette (left). Near Chadds Ford, in the
fieldstone Gilpin House (above), the marquis made his headquarters. On September 11, Howe crossed the Brandywine
upstream, outflanked Washington, and defeated him deci-
sively. Lafayette fought hard, but took a bullet in the leg.

Indian trick in that wilderness theater of war. Knowing that the Indians held a superstitious faith in the words of madmen and idiots, Arnold sent an addled messenger into St. Leger's camp. The messenger babbled that Americans were coming in great numbers; St. Leger's Indians firmly believed him. Many fled in panic; others insisted on retreat. St. Leger fell back, halted by trickery.

What idiotic babbling did to St. Leger, a change of mind did to General Howe, by now a Knight of the Bath and, properly, Sir William. He left New York—but not to meet Burgoyne on the upper Hudson. Instead, he put Sir Henry Clinton in charge at New York and sailed toward "the first object," as Howe wrote, "Philadelphia... capital, as it were, and residence of the Congress...."

HOWE LANDED his troops at Head of Elk on Chesapeake Bay. "To bring the enemy to an action was my object," wrote Howe. "... General Washington was studious to avoid it unless under most favorable circumstances...."

Washington felt he had those circumstances as he waited on the east bank of beautiful Brandywine Creek. On September 11, British units across the stream had opened a bombardment when Washington heard that Howe had made "a terrible blunder" by dividing his force and sending a column off northward. Boldly Washington ordered the same blunder—he told Greene to cross the creek and attack the redcoats there, and he sent two divisions out to see what Howe's northbound column might be up to.

But the British blunder was really Sir William's ruse, and his marching brigades had turned to threaten the American rear. Troops of the unlucky Sullivan rushed to stop them but ran into the glinting steel of British bayonets. Surprise turned to confusion and the Americans' frantically improvised line sagged and wavered. Washington and Greene galloped their horses to the new front where 3,000 Americans still held high ground against some 6,000 British and Germans under the able Cornwallis.

So fierce was the firing that Philadelphians could hear the guns 25 miles away. One bullet struck the leg of the eager Lafayette, just turned 20 and in his first battle. He faced the enemy with easy courage until blood ran out of the top of his boot.

With equal—and desperate—courage the Americans clung to the high ground. But as the sun went down the inevitable came about. They retreated in disorder, with Greene fighting a staunch rear-guard action, to join comrades driven back from the stream's banks.

Brandywine was another American defeat. Howe had again turned Washington's flank, just as he had on Long Island. Some 300 Americans had died; perhaps 400 were taken prisoner. Wilmington promptly fell. But Brandywine was not a rout. Washington had kept his army intact.

One recent September, as I chauffeured Kel to his school in western Massachusetts, we stopped off to see the quiet Brandywine Creek on the anniversary of its battle. Then we headed north, marking our latitude by the changing color of foliage. When we reached the upper Hudson, we had swapped a tired summer for a fresh fall. Frost had touched the tips of hilltop maples, apples in the valleys were fat and red, and whole green mountainsides had begun to rust. We called it "Burgoyne's weather," for Handsome Jack was still on the upper Hudson that week in 1777.

Of those planned expeditions in upstate New York, only Burgoyne's could be found. Supplies had run short, so he sent a German raiding party into the newly declared republic of Vermont seeking food and more horses. But Gen. John Stark and the militia completely vanquished the slow-moving Germans at Bennington, killing 200 men and taking some 700 prisoners.

Now way behind schedule, a bulky train limped along on land while a motley flotilla of river craft moved downstream. Summer leaves were paling. Bennington had cost Burgoyne time as well as men. His Indians, closely restricted after the murder of Jane McCrea, held a council of war, and all but about 80 went home. Burgoyne could now count only about 6,300 men.

Militia by the hundreds flocked to join Gen. Horatio Gates, commanding the Americans at Albany. There he had gathered a force of 7,000, including Arnold's men, back from the Mohawk valley, and the riflemen

Young Jane McCrea, fiancée of a Tory lieutenant, struggles helplessly in the hands of two of Burgoyne's Indians. Americans blamed the fierce Wyandots for murdering and scalping her, a charge that provided fuel for propagandists. Volunteers turned out for vengeance on Burgoyne.

of Daniel Morgan, freed by an exchange of prisoners. On September 12, Gates and his chief engineer, the able Kosciuszko, began to lay out defenses on Bemis Heights.

Modern visitors who walk along these 200-foot, wind-washed bluffs can see how narrowly the Bemis Heights squeeze the Hudson valley—enough for 18th-century cannon to halt an army train and its river fleet. Standing there, we watched a long, low oil barge slip past at a tugboat's pace; not a hundred yards away, cars sped on a highway that follows the old historic road. This was the last narrow neck of the bottle. If Burgoyne had moved past Bemis Heights, Albany and the northern Hudson should have been his.

On September 19, 1777, Burgoyne made his first try; three widely separated columns advanced. Near the cleared land of Freeman's Farm, the British heard the eerie gobble of wild turkeys—a true forest noise, but this time made by the frontiersmen under Morgan. Perched in treetops, camouflaged in their hunting shirts, the Americans kept a perpetual watch on the redcoats.

Toward midday, the hidden rifles fired on a band of General Burgoyne's men just north of Freeman's Farm.

From high ground above that farm—land once forested but today cleared and gently sloping—the modern visitor commands a view more nearly complete than any general

Steaming in a chill Saratoga sunrise, the Hudson River flows deep and narrow just upstream from Bemis Heights, where General Burgoyne's army advanced from Canada toward Albany to join Howe's command. But American Gen. Horatio Gates fortified the banks and stopped Burgoyne here. After two battles, the British held out bravely but briefly on their hilltop Balcarres Redoubt (below). The author's wife and children compare terrain with battle maps prepared by the Saratoga National Historical Park.

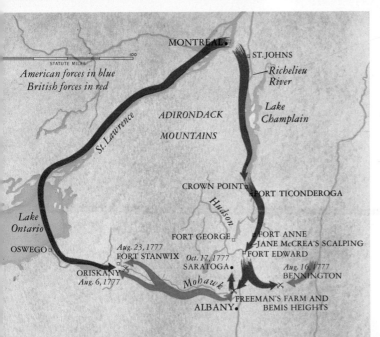

STATUTE MILES   100

American forces in blue
British forces in red

MONTREAL
ST. JOHNS
Richelieu River
Lake Champlain
ADIRONDACK MOUNTAINS
St. Lawrence
CROWN POINT
FORT TICONDEROGA
Hudson
Lake Ontario
FORT GEORGE
FORT ANNE
JANE McCREA'S SCALPING
OSWEGO
Aug. 23, 1777
FORT STANWIX
FORT EDWARD
Oct. 17, 1777
SARATOGA
Aug. 16, 1777
BENNINGTON
ORISKANY
Aug. 6, 1777
Mohawk
FREEMAN'S FARM AND
BEMIS HEIGHTS
ALBANY

British scissors might have snipped the rebel states in two: Burgoyne's route from Montreal led to the Hudson. Lt. Col. Barry St. Leger would move via the St. Lawrence and Lake Ontario to take Fort Stanwix, then meet Burgoyne. British troops from Manhattan would make a diversion on the Hudson. But plans went awry. St. Leger besieged Fort Stanwix. His Indians ambushed militia at Oriskany, but he retreated before Arnold's advance north of the Mohawk. Howe went to Philadelphia; and Burgoyne surrendered at Saratoga.

117

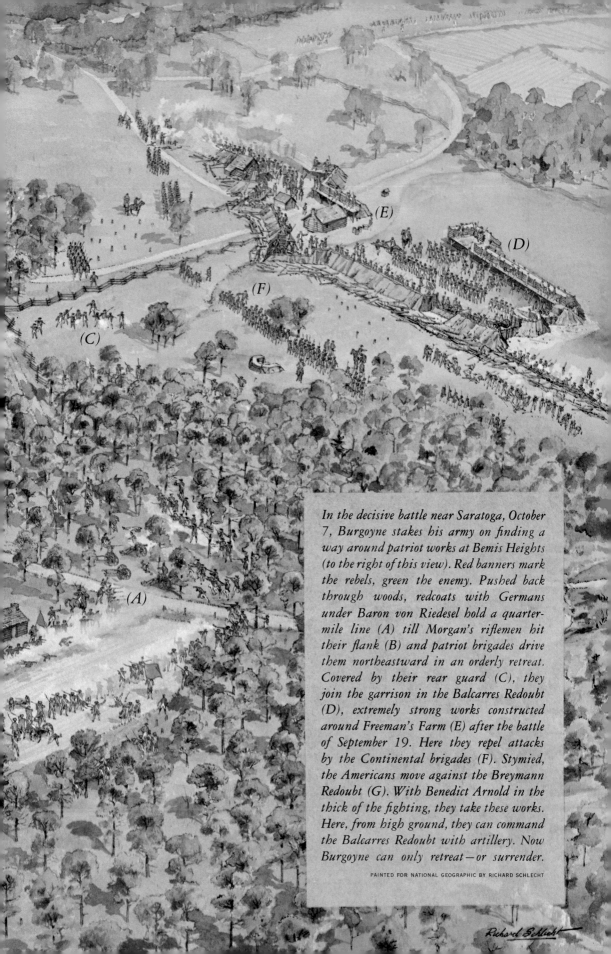

(E)

(D)

(F)

(C)

(A)

In the decisive battle near Saratoga, October 7, Burgoyne stakes his army on finding a way around patriot works at Bemis Heights (to the right of this view). Red banners mark the rebels, green the enemy. Pushed back through woods, redcoats with Germans under Baron von Riedesel hold a quarter-mile line (A) till Morgan's riflemen hit their flank (B) and patriot brigades drive them northeastward in an orderly retreat. Covered by their rear guard (C), they join the garrison in the Balcarres Redoubt (D), extremely strong works constructed around Freeman's Farm (E) after the battle of September 19. Here they repel attacks by the Continental brigades (F). Stymied, the Americans move against the Breymann Redoubt (G). With Benedict Arnold in the thick of the fighting, they take these works. Here, from high ground, they can command the Balcarres Redoubt with artillery. Now Burgoyne can only retreat—or surrender.

PAINTED FOR NATIONAL GEOGRAPHIC BY RICHARD SCHLECHT

Richard Schlecht

PAINTING BY HOWARD SMITH, CONTINENTAL INSURANCE COMPANY

saw in 1777. We could easily find the spot where Morgan's men pursued the retreating enemy—and where Morgan was pulled up short: The Americans had advanced in form-less zest—and now themselves were charged and scattered. Dan Morgan was left alone and furious in the forest—to gobble-call his men and to re-form.

They did re-form, and others with them. Arnold's men fought with their leader's dash, and the 20-acre farm changed hands time and again. British losses were fearful; only the arrival of the German von Riedesel saved the day from disaster. As the redcoats fell, the Brunswickers came up, their feet pounding to a steady double-time drumbeat, to open

fire on the Yankees with a yell of "Hurrah!"

In the gathering darkness, the Americans withdrew, and the British bivouacked with symbolic victory on Freeman's Farm. Less victoriously, they counted 600 killed, wounded, and captured—twice the loss of the Americans.

Perhaps that night Burgoyne recalled the expensive victory of Bunker Hill; in any case, his prose grows less purple and more blue: "From the 20th of September to the 7th of October, the armies were so near, that not a night passed without firing. . . . I do not believe that either officer or soldier ever slept . . . without his cloaths. . . ."

Hoarfrost shone on the reddened sugar

ing the von Riedesel journal as we drove around the Saratoga environs. And as Martha read, three-year-old Rob napped in her lap; I think the baroness would have approved of Martha, too. "...suddenly on October 7 my husband...had to break camp....I heard. ...a terrible bombardment...."

Burgoyne was now attempting a "reconnaissance in force," trying to find a way around the American roadblock. It was then that Gates told Dan Morgan to "begin the game."

The most dramatic figure on the battlefield that day was Benedict Arnold. He had quarreled with Gates and had been left without a command. Impulsively he grabbed a big bay horse and dashed onto the field of war. A man without fear, Arnold seemed to be everywhere, inspiring his compatriots, urging fierce assaults upon the British redoubts, a wild and reckless figure—until a bullet struck his left leg. He lived to fight again—but not for the United States.

Now a brave Briton on a gray horse was fatally cut down; he was General Fraser, and his fall dispirited his comrades. Darkness settled upon another British disaster of 600 killed, wounded, and captured. Strong points had fallen with the strong-hearted.

In a cold rainstorm the British retired to the village of Saratoga, and the Baroness von Riedesel set out for a house perched above the Hudson. "A terrifying cannonade" arrived as her carriage pulled up to the house: "I thrust my children onto the floor...and threw myself over them...."

When they could go indoors, she found that "the house contained only the wounded and women!...Eleven cannon balls flew through the house, and we could distinctly hear them rolling about....One of the poor soldiers who lay on a table, and was just about to have his leg amputated, had the other leg shot off by one of these balls."

That house of refuge still stands, the private home of Mrs. T. K. Bullard, a gracious person who asked our children, "Would you like to see the same cannon balls that the

maples and the gilded oaks. And as the autumn scenery brightened, so did American prospects. Gates's army was growing daily until more than 9,500 Americans were mustered in this wilderness. More thousands of militiamen threatened Burgoyne's line of retreat. The Baroness von Riedesel—traveling in a carriage with her three daughters—recalled: "the country was magnificent, but... all the people had...gone to strengthen the American army....every inhabitant is a born soldier and a good marksman; in addition, the thought of fighting for...freedom made them braver than ever."

My wife Martha approved. "A good woman, the baroness," she said. Martha was read-

baroness heard?" Mrs. Bullard also showed us bloodstains on her parlor floor.

"From that man's *leg?*" asked Josh. Mrs. Bullard assured him solemnly that they were the same. Yet for Martha and me, several old white pines on the front lawn seemed the most remarkable monuments. They were veterans of that Battle of Saratoga — and still alive.

Burgoyne waited until surrender was his only recourse. Then he tried to save face, by calling his capitulation a "convention." Handsome Jack Burgoyne rode out in his best uniform to the American camp and addressed Horatio Gates: "The fortune of war, General Gates, has made me your prisoner."

Yet Burgoyne himself wrote a better curtain speech for his romantic drama *Richard Cœur de Lion:* "And when to my native England I return, so may I . . . cherish . . . a lesson to improve my reign: compassion should be a monarch's nature. I have learned what 'tis to need it. . . ."

Exit Burgoyne.

It was my 15-year-old son Kel who found another teen-ager's reaction to Saratoga: "we got news of the defeat of General Burgoine [sic]," wrote young Hugh McDonald, a North Carolina lad who became a soldier at 14. ". . . we rejoiced with great shouting and firing all day, our officers being more joyous than the common soldiers. . . ."

Hugh McDonald's friends needed a celebration. After Brandywine, all the Pennsylvania news had been bad. Swashbuckling Gen. Anthony Wayne had been overwhelmed in the dead of night only a few miles from his ancestral home; there at Paoli the British had again used the bayonet with devastating success, killing and capturing at least 200 men as against a loss of less than a dozen.

Colonial home that served as a British hospital overlooks the Hudson River near Schuylerville, New York. The Baroness von Riedesel, wife of German Maj. Gen. Frederick von Riedesel, took refuge inside with her three daughters during the cannonade of Saratoga. "We had no water ..." the baroness wrote, "because the enemy shot every man in the head who went near the river." American snipers finally permitted a soldier's wife to run to the river, down the slope where the author and his family stroll. The von Riedesels (below) became prisoners of war after Burgoyne's surrender.

"Why do they call it the Paoli *Massacre?*" Kel asked. "It was a battle fair and square. The British slipped up on us, and we fought back all right."

True enough. But Paoli gave Wayne something to brood about.

Less than a week later General Howe entered Philadelphia, "that Mass of Cowardice and Toryism," as John Adams called it. Congress fled to Lancaster, Pennsylvania.

George Washington now planned revenge, perhaps too carefully. I tried to explain his Germantown plan to the children as we drove along School House Lane; Washington would divide his force into four columns for a giant, double pincer that would close on Howe's 9,000 men encamped at Germantown. The columns would march at night and attack in unison with a bayonet charge; the men would wear bits of white paper on their hats for easy recognition. But the plan was entirely too sophisticated for a half-trained army. Greene's column went astray and arrived late. Fog turned the battlefield into a milky mystery.

Some of the British gathered in a square stone mansion on Skippack Road: the Chew House. We stopped there briefly to pace off a lawn where 53 Americans died.

Washington's men repeatedly tried to dislodge the defenders. They failed, the firing roused the British, plans went awry.

And withal, Washington almost won. At one point, Howe himself ran out and shouted to rally his light infantry: "Form! Form! I never saw you retreat before!"

Finally, blinded by fog, the Americans were even firing at each other. Yet, as Tom Paine reported, their "retreat was extraordinary. Nobody hurried themselves."

Its lawn watered with the blood of 53 Americans, the Chew House bristles as a British fortress at Germantown, near Philadelphia, where Washington hoped for a victory after Brandywine. Failure to take the mansion upset the timing of the battle plan and forced a retreat. Young Rob McDowell (right) deploys his toy soldiers on the now quiet grounds.

PAINTING BY HOWARD PYLE, WILMINGTON SOCIETY OF THE FINE ARTS, DELAWARE ART CENTER; AND NATIONAL GEOGRAPHIC PHOTOGRAPHER JAMES L. STANFIELD

They were deeply tired, and so were the British. But this hard-fought, murky battle won both respect and time for the attackers. General Howe would not pursue the Americans soon. Wrote he: "The intrenched situation of the enemy at Valley-Forge, twenty-two miles from Philadelphia, did not . . . justify an attack upon that strong post during the severe weather . . . I judged it imprudent . . . I dropped all thoughts of an attack. . . ."

The crucial, lonely year was drawing to a quiet end. Trenton had convinced Americans they could win. Saratoga was convincing the French. Now, in London, old Horace Walpole logged his diary thus: "At the end of the year died Dr. Frederick Keppel, Bishop of Exeter and Dean of Windsor. On his deathbed he thanked God that he had not given one vote for shedding American blood.

"End of the year 1777."

125

In winter camp at Valley Forge, His Excellency General Washington rides out with his aides to review

1778:
"Princes of the Earth"

...he troops still able to march for him—men face to face with cold, disease, starvation, and despair.

VALLEY FORGE seemed false when we saw it in the green, ripe summer. We jostled along with a great crowd of visitors like ourselves —tots dragging toys, parents bangled with cameras. All of us turned the grassy slopes into a noisy picnic park; without meaning to, we trespassed upon the mood of history.

"But that's the way the British saw it," said Tina. And she was quite right. General Howe's foraging parties came through the valley in the autumn of 1777 and stripped a bountiful countryside of food and wagons.

Since we could not trust our summertime impressions, we returned in the winter to sample its seasonal bite. The valley lay beneath a heavy snow, "just the way Washington's men saw it!" said Josh excitedly. In all honesty I had to straighten the record. That winter of 1777-78 was not severely cold.

"Had there fallen deep snows...the whole army must inevitably have perished," wrote Pvt. Joseph Martin. Hunger was the greater danger. "We arrived at the Valley Forge in the evening.... I lay here two nights and one day and had not a morsel of anything to eat ...save half of a small pumpkin...." The same

127

Washington's arrival." The same accounts, estimating Pennsylvania shillings by present-day prices, showed butter selling for $1.51 a pound and tea for twenty times that amount —when available. There was no wonder that the army went hungry.

Dr. Albigence Waldo, of Connecticut, recorded in his diary the daily menu: "Fire cake and water, sir.... The Lord send that our Commissary of Purchases may live on fire cake and water till their glutted guts are turned to pasteboard."

Josh felt that we should at least taste fire cake, and Tina agreed to cook it. But we could never find a real recipe for Valley Forge fire cake. It was probably a soggy, chewy mess of flour paste baked on a hot stone; fire cake had no leavening and little if any salt (salt was painfully scarce during the Revolution). "Nobody saves a recipe like that," said Tina. "Thank goodness."

The privations were as varied as they were severe: On one occasion, of the 9,000 troops one-fourth were reported unfit for duty "because they are bare foot and otherwise naked." Smallpox broke out, and typhus— called the "putrid fever"—took an even

soldier celebrated a Continental Thanksgiving decreed by the Congress with "half a gill of rice and a tablespoonful of vinegar!!"

In the local museum, the children saw Washington's tent. "He slept in that?" Tina asked. He did, until all his men had log huts to sleep in. Then Washington moved into an attractive fieldstone farmhouse down the road. Martha Washington soon joined him, as she did each winter of the war.

"But look at these Valley Forge household accounts," said my own Martha. "Here they bought five new brooms, just before Martha

Washington ordered all 900 log cabins "made tight with Clay" for winter warmth. Until his men got shelter, the general slept in a canvas marquee. "I was there when the Army began to build huts," wrote Thomas Paine, ". . . like a family of beavers. . . ." Below, youngsters sled on slopes around the "artillery park," among 25 copies of the 4-pounders that General Knox brought here.

larger toll. One officer noted that "horses are dying for want of forage." Some 500 rotting carcasses fouled the whole camp.

No wonder that men deserted and sought employment with the British in Philadelphia, or that some officers murmured about the "Conway Cabal"—they feared a plot to replace George Washington with the hero of Saratoga, Horatio Gates.

Washington might hang a deserter, but when he suspected intrigue, he moved with subtlety. Congress still appointed all general officers, but Washington maneuvered men he trusted into posts that mattered.

Nathanael Greene, as the new Quartermaster General, would get food and clothing to the men. He proved as hard as his father's anvil; Greene's motto became "Forage the country naked!" His raiders seized cattle,

or slaughtered them lest the British find them later.

On our own winter visit to Valley Forge, we saw snowdrifts standing roof-high beside the log huts now reconstructed in the valley. With every thaw or shower, the low, steep hills must have turned the bottomland to bog. We could imagine the difficulties of the men as they dragged wagons through muddy ruts or searched out a parade ground for drill.

American mythology has largely crowded out the great value of Valley Forge as a time of preparation. On February 23, 1778, it became a training field—part boot camp, part war college—for on that day Baron von Steuben arrived. He appeared as a German nobleman; he was undoubtedly a tough, professional, German warrior, age 47. He spoke little English, except for one

Baron von Steuben, in the finery of a Prussian officer and the service of the U.S.A., gives a lesson in his method of handling muskets for more volleys per minute. By the time the Continental Army left Valley Forge, he had drilled the men thoroughly in marching, bayonet tactics, and other arts of war. One of Washington's soldiers, John Cotton, whittled these chessmen in his hours off duty.

explosive oath that he saved for the drill field.

The Baron looked over the suffering men, some "literally naked . . . in the fullest extent of the word." No European army, he said, could have held together in such circumstances. "With regard to military discipline," he added, ". . . no such thing existed."

Therewith, he sat down to write a drillbook in French. His secretary translated it; John Laurens and Alexander Hamilton edited it. Von Steuben became a drillmaster himself; the great Prussian "condescended" to act as a sergeant, one astonished officer wrote his family. Thus the Prussian changed the army attitude with his "plate of *sauerkraut,*" as he called it. His language problems made the irreverent Americans laugh, so that Inspector General von Steuben quickly became one of the army's most popular personalities.

And what he taught! Units heretofore had marched in a sloppy, strung-out, Indian fashion; now easy-stepping men advanced compactly, four abreast — and the whole army suddenly moved faster. Von Steuben found that half the men lacked bayonets and others used the blades only in cooking. So the men drilled daily with the bayonet. Von Steuben also brought a new professional pride, just as important as his manual of arms. He became the American substitute for all those competent British army sergeants who made the enemy outfits work. By late March, Washington wrote that "our prospects begin to brighten."

Yet enormous problems remained. Prices were rising and Continental money was falling in value; notes counterfeited by the British were circulating widely. Soon Americans would be trading in 17 sorts of money,

Defending home waters for the first time in the war, a British fleet battles the French off Ushant

PAINTING BY G. L. GANNÉ AFTER THEODORE GUDIN, UNITED STATES NAVAL ACADEMY MUSEUM

uly 27. On opposite courses, they exchange broadsides. The French left their foe hurt but unbeaten.

and even using lottery tickets as currency.

The war brought personal worries to Washington. His stepson John Parke Custis was selling lands in southeastern Virginia to buy 2,000 acres near Mount Vernon—a place today known as Arlington National Cemetery. As Jack collected paper money, the general warned him to reinvest it at once or "it will melt like Snow before a hot Sun."

Then there was his Tory neighbor Bryan Fairfax. Sick at heart, Fairfax had tried to join the British in New York but he had ended up in jail at Lancaster, Pennsylvania.

Washington sent his old friend a safe-conduct pass across American lines—on his word not to divulge secrets to the British. The gesture, wrote Fairfax, "hath affected me more than any Favour I have received...." In New York, Fairfax became disillusioned with the British, so he returned to Virginia sadly, a man between countries.

In the dreary rain of early springtime, 1778, the American cause moved slowly. Congress was writing the Articles of Confederation. Washington's aide Alexander Hamilton took time to criticize those early drafts. Nathanael Greene kept to his account books and learned the useful arts of logistics and supply. And perhaps an obscure young Virginian named John Marshall, as he ate Valley Forge fire cake, gave some abstract thought to governments with strength enough to levy taxes and feed their armies.

On the morning of April 30, Washington was still discouraged enough to write in one letter, "our present situation... is beyond description, irksome and dangerous." Then, in his afternoon mail, he found, as he told his army, that "the Almighty ruler of the Universe" was "raising us up a powerful Friend among the Princes of the Earth." On February 6, France had recognized the independence of the United States. The step meant a French war against Great Britain. The thirteen somewhat United States were no longer alone.

Once again, for an instant, the marble mask drops away: We see George Washington playing—yes, playing with some youngsters of his army—a game of wickets on the grass.

The whole army celebrated in proper fashion on Tuesday, May 6. Baron von Steuben prepared the parade. The cannon fired symbolic 13-gun salutes, and the whole army shouted in a single explosive baritone:

Sword held high, Washington rallies his men in the swirling confusion near Monmouth Courthouse; Gen. Charles Lee, rebuked for a disorderly retreat, slumps on his white charger. The Continentals had caught up with British columns lumbering across New Jersey toward New York. Under Washington's eye they fought the red-coats to a standstill in the open field. Leutze's romantic canvas, 23 by 13 feet, lay forgotten for half a century in a basement at the University of California at Berkeley. In 1965 Herschel B. Chipp of the school's art gallery found it rolled around a redwood log, and put it on display.

"Huzza! Long Live the King of France!" After the review Washington started back to his quarters. Suddenly he stopped, and in a voice usually raised only for command, he yelled loud enough to send an echo through the valley: "Huzza! Huzza! Huzza!"

By quirk of events, Sir Henry Clinton was at that very moment sailing from New York to Philadelphia. There he relieved the high-living Sir William Howe and took charge as His Majesty's Commander-in-Chief for the American theater. The Howe brothers still had time, though, for a gala goodbye.

Not far from town, at the Wharton estate, the Tories and Britons held an extravagant pageant, feast, and ball. The talented dandy Capt. John André, who designed the ladies' costumes and coiffures, called this party the "Mischianza," or Medley. Beautiful Tory girls posed as "the Ladies of the Blended Rose" or "of the Burning Mountain" while play-like knights tilted in their honor.

But Lord Howe's sensible secretary Ambrose Serle felt that "Our Enemies will dwell upon the Folly and Extravagance...with Pleasure." Again, Serle was right. And the show seemed all the sillier when British soldiers packed up to abandon Philadelphia.

PAINTING BY EMANUEL LEUTZE, 1854, COLLECTION OF THE UNIVERSITY ART MUSEUM OF THE UNIVERSITY OF CALIFORNIA, BERKELEY, GIFT OF MRS. MARK HOPKINS

Their capture of the city had failed to paralyze the American war effort. The king's loyal Tories had given only tepid help. Aggressive loyalist sentiment—sought first in New England, then in New York, the Jerseys, and Philadelphia—was still to be found.

At 3 a.m. on June 18, the last of Clinton's army of 11,000 men left Philadelphia, and a race began with Washington's forces. Once the spring plowing was done, sunshine patriots had increased his strength dramatically: to some 13,500 men. Better fed, but still lightly dressed, the Continentals now found light packs a blessing, for Washington wanted to overtake Clinton and attack his rear guard.

The British staggered and sweated. Smartly and swelteringly uniformed, they marched through deep sand, carrying heavy packs, lending a shoulder when needed to 1,500 wagons, a baggage train 12 miles long. They took 6 days to plod 30 miles. The cooler, less encumbered Americans covered nearly 50 miles in the same time.

NEAR MONMOUTH COURTHOUSE—in an area of sand, swamp, and forest—on the early morning of June 28, American units caught up with Clinton. By Washington's orders, but at his own request, Gen. Charles Lee—now exchanged from British captivity—led the attack. Washington himself was bringing up the main force when "to my great surprise and mortification," he wrote later, "I met the whole advanced Corps retreating."

Men on horseback and others on foot scrambled through muggy ravines and through the splintering blindness in airless woods. Written orders went awry; shouted orders were drowned in noise. Washington met Lee and angrily demanded an explanation.

"Sir, sir?" sputtered Lee. And then followed a much-described, much-disputed dialogue. One officer said long afterward that General Washington "swore that day till the leaves shook on the trees."

At the very least, Charles Lee was shaken. This was his last battle.

Now George Washington, angry as an avenging angel, personally halted the retreat. Conspicuously he rode the huge white horse given him by New Jersey's governor until the exhausted mount fell dead. He was everywhere, as Lafayette later told it, "all along the lines amid the shouts of the soldiers, cheering them by his voice and example and restoring

... the fortunes of the fight. I thought then, as now, that never had I beheld so superb a man."

The sweltering battle raged with multiple attacks. Washington recalled the "extreme heat of the Weather, the fatigue of the men from their march thro' a deep, sandy Country almost entirely destitute of Water."

Sir Henry Clinton logged a similar complaint: "Besides those slain ... the heat of the day destroyed us fifty-nine more...."

From such horrible heat came the heroism of "Molly Pitcher," a name attached to other women water-bearers. At Monmouth, tradition has it, thirsty men gratefully blessed the pitcher of Mary Hayes, who also found time to use a gun.

The battle died away as the sun went down; darkness and exhaustion enforced a truce. Men lay on their arms; Washington spread his own cloak beneath an oak tree. All the warriors rested until "near mid-night," as Sir Henry told it, when the king's troops "took advantage of the coolness of the night to escape the fatal effects of another day's sun, and resumed their march...."

On a long summer evening, we watched darkness fall on the orchards, the golf course, and the railroad tracks that pattern the sprawling Monmouth landscape today. Its broken terrain helped to show why neither side won a clear victory. But other records were clearly established in 1778: Monmouth was the war's longest and hottest battle—and the last large engagement in the north.

At the summer moment of Monmouth, we can listen to new noises and faster rhythms of a war changing in mood. New sounds come with the animated talk of Frenchmen, the clank and bump of cannon a-loading on ships, and the creak of rigging as great fleets sail. No longer does this revolt seem a family quarrel. Suddenly the war grows vast and exotic.

"Look at the Fourth of July in 1778!" exclaimed Josh once, consulting the war calendar on our family bulletin board. "We had a surrender and a victory on the same day!" These weren't the great encounters of formal

"Molly Pitcher," heroine of Monmouth, catches up a rammer to load a cannon where her husband has fallen in the sweltering heat. Mary Hayes won her famous nickname carrying water to hard-pressed and wounded troops. Strong and tough as any other veteran, she survived until 1832.

War whoops ring among cries of anguish as the patriot defenders of the Susquehanna valley fall to the tomahawks of Iroquois and Tory Rangers —bitterly remembered as "blue-eyed Indians"— in the "Wyoming Massacre" of July 3 and 4. The loyalist commander reported his men had taken 227 scalps from men struck down in the battle.

armies. But their widely separated frontier sites reveal the war's new dimensions.

Near modern Wilkes-Barre, Pennsylvania, into the Wyoming valley of the Susquehanna River, slipped a stealthy force of perhaps 1,100 men. They were a mixture of Tory Rangers and fierce Iroquois Indians. They surrounded and defeated the small patriot garrison; then fearful rumor had it that they ran amok in an orgy of blood. Prisoners were burned to death—men were held in the fire with pitchforks, went the legends. In this "Wyoming Massacre" of July 3 and 4, His Majesty's savages took 227 rebel scalps.

But on the same day, 800 miles west, at Kaskaskia in the Illinois country, a tall frontiersman from Virginia led a band of 175 men through the wilderness. This was George Rogers Clark, surveyor, Indian fighter, and patriot. His men had not eaten in two days; they would, quite simply, have to find food at the enemy village of Kaskaskia. But their very audacity saved them; the town was totally surprised. And the French settlers of this British-owned outpost surrendered without a shot. The Revolution had reached the mud of the Mississippi.

One week later, the Revolution became an Atlantic naval war: Twelve French ships of the line, four frigates, and attendant vessels— a heavily armed flotilla carrying 4,000 French troops—appeared off New York. For eleven days the commander of this fleet, Charles Hector Théodat, the proud Count d'Estaing, waited outside New York harbor. But his magnificent ships had too deep a draft to cross the bar, and Admiral Lord Howe kept his outgunned squadron behind it.

Next, d'Estaing sailed north to Rhode Island to join John Sullivan's operation against a British force at Newport. Friction quickly developed between the blunt Sullivan and the courtly nobleman from the Old World.

On August 9, Sullivan heard that the British had abandoned a key position. The Americans were grabbing this opportunity, and

Sullivan asked d'Estaing to land his French troops. But just then Lord Howe's reinforced fleet arrived, gravely threatening the allied operation. For two days, the two admirals gambled on shifting winds and maneuvered for position. The wind finally changed—but insanely: A two-day gale scattered all the ships like chaff and damaged both fleets. Howe limped off to New York, and d'Estaing said he, too, was leaving.

Sullivan again appealed for French help, but the Count was moody. Could d'Estaing stay just 24 hours? He refused. Off he sailed to Boston with his 4,000 French troops, leaving Sullivan to go it alone.

The discouraged American militia was decimated by desertions—5,000 left in a few days—so Sullivan could consider nothing but retreat. Even retreat was dangerous under

the new pressure of the British and Hessians. All too few of Sullivan's men had been under fire. And some were unknown quantities— like Col. Christopher Greene's Rhode Island unit of free Negroes. The cool, professional Hessians confidently attacked Greene's regiment. But the Negroes showed a "desperate valor," as Sullivan's biographer Thomas Amory told it. Three times they turned back the Hessians' charge.

Finally, after a hot exchange of fire, night came—and with it came a familiar cast: John Glover's Marblehead sailors "who so cheerfully turned out," said the orderly book, to ferry their fellow Americans to safety.

Yet a bitter aftertaste lingered around Count d'Estaing and the new French allies. Historically hotheaded Boston welcomed the French fleet in September with curiosity, suspicion—and one ugly incident. The French set up a bakery ashore to supply their ships. Since flour had vanished from the Boston market, a crowd of local people tried to buy French bread. The baker spoke no English, the Bostonians no French. Misunderstanding turned to anger, then to a riotous street fight. In the disturbance, a young French lieutenant, the Chevalier de Saint-Sauveur, was killed.

Could the infant alliance survive the murder of a highborn officer? With great tact, the episode was brushed aside and even blamed on the absent British. But in another way the incident made history: Saint-Sauveur's funeral, conducted by a Franciscan priest in a nearly secret ceremony, was quite possibly the first Roman Catholic Mass ever said in Boston. America's foreign friends had already brought more than a wider war.

Side by side, H.M.S. Serapis *(foreground) and* Bonhomme Richard *fight the most spectacular due*

1779-80: "With Unremitting Fury"

of the war, off the British coast in 1779. The victor: America's first great naval hero, John Paul Jones.

THE CONTEMPORARY TRAVELER who flies in to Savannah, Georgia, can easily see the region's military temptations. The colonial town sat on a defensible bluff, but surrounding marshes and pine-covered plains still isolate the city. The Atlantic Ocean and the navigable Savannah River invite an invasion fleet.

The British accepted such an invitation at Christmastime of 1778. Lt. Col. Archibald Campbell sent scouts ashore on Christmas night "in two Flat-boats . . . to seize any of the

Inhabitants they might find on the Banks" for military intelligence. The scouts succeeded, and Campbell felt sure his 3,500 troops could take the river port. Two days later they did. The British lost only 7 killed. But at least 83 Americans died and 453 were captured. The shattered American survivors fled to join Gen. Benjamin Lincoln in South Carolina. Thus Campbell made a Christmas prophecy for 1779 and beyond: The war had turned south—and turned ugly.

This switch in direction had good reason. With the northern campaign in stalemate, the British still hoped to find in the South those "good Americans to subdue the bad ones," as one of their generals put it. On the specific orders of Lord George Germain, Sir Henry Clinton had dispatched this fleet.

Thus the British waged their civil war with a march through Georgia. Fort Sunbury fell on January 10, Augusta by January 31.... For a time, the British even propped up a royal legislature in Georgia, the only one to meet after the Declaration of Independence.

"That doesn't really count," said Kel. "Georgia only had 50,000 people—and half of them were slaves. Besides, the patriots were still fighting."

Those Georgia patriots with Capt. John Dooley got some revenge on St. Valentine's Day. With Col. Andrew Pickens's South Carolinians, they caught a Tory force at Kettle Creek. His Majesty's loyal subjects were butchering stolen beef when Pickens surprised them. An hour later, 40 Tories were dead, 75 captured, and the rest scattered.

Kettle Creek was a tonic to southern patriotism, but it left one nasty stain: The prisoners were dragged off to South Carolina, tried for treason, and—70 of them—sentenced to die. Most were pardoned, but five of these luckless Tory prisoners were indeed hanged in the name of freedom. Somehow this incident typifies the small, mean battles—the compressed, fratricidal bitterness—of the southern campaign.

On the western frontier, for all the savagery of Indian fighting, the war could be different: expansive, adventurous, and sometimes even fun. When I mentioned this to Tina, she seemed shocked. Then I told her a little

The war moves west to the Illinois country, held by the British and their Indian allies. It covered a vast wilderness south of the Great Lakes.

Frontiersmen led by George Rogers Clark wade for miles through icy Wabash floods to surprise the British at Vincennes in February, 1779. A bronze statue of Clark (right) at Vincennes, Indiana, stands before a mural of the successful attack. The country he fought for came under the American flag by treaty at the end of the war.

ARCHIVES OF AMERICAN ART, DETROIT, AND TERRILL E. EILER (OPPOSITE)

about George Rogers Clark, a colonel who knew how to lead his men with laughter.

Clark's whole 1,200-mile wilderness march in 1778 and 1779 has the wild quality of a Western tall tale. This lean, ruddy Virginian —just 26 in 1779—deliberately chose a Strategy of the Absurd.

An enemy party from Detroit had occupied the fort at Vincennes. Clark took 127 men 180 miles from Kaskaskia to attack Vincennes because the British "could not suppose ... we should be so mad as to attempt to march 80 Leagues through a Drownded Cuntry in the Debth of Wintor," as Clark wrote in a memoir. "my object now was to keep the men in spirits I suffered them to shoot game ... and feast like Indians ... each company by Turns Inviteing the other to their feasts. ... Thus ... without a Murmur was those men led on the Banks of the Little Wabash ... through Increditable difficulties. ..."

The Wabash made a single flooded expanse 20 miles across. Clark's men waded. "A little antick Drummer afforded them great diversion by floating on his Drum. ..." (I read this portion to young Rob—and then regretted it: He wanted to take his own drum to the swimming pool and try the same trick.)

So Clark's fun-loving men splashed on, sometimes shoulder deep, enduring the cold and the wet and finally hunger. After 17 days, they reached Vincennes.

And then, while carefully concealing his scant number, Colonel Clark surprised his enemy utterly by an unthinkable ruse: He sent a letter to the town announcing his presence and his confidence in victory. Clark's wily use of the truth actually worked. The pro-American townsmen withheld their help from the British fort; the Indian allies of the British simply ran away.

Clark demanded surrender of the despised Briton, Lt. Col. Henry Hamilton, a man called the Hair Buyer by patriots for his reputed purchase of American scalps. The confrontation came after a night of siege. Coldly, Clark demanded "Mr Hamiltons surrendering himself and Garrison." And now Clark

Carried by aides, the wounded Gen. "Mad Anthony" Wayne directs a bayonet attack up the fortified promontory (left) of Stony Point, New York. His men stormed the stronghold by night, in July, 1779, a victory that heartened the nation. Wayne's nickname remains a byword for daring.

knew the time had come to end all laughter. For the cruel benefit of his enemy, he brought forward Indian prisoners who had been caught carrying American scalps. Clark's men executed the Indians by tomahawk in full view of the Hair Buyer. Hamilton and his fort promptly surrendered. And so George Rogers Clark won the Illinois frontier; its French settlers gave their allegiance to the American flag, and remained loyal.

BY THE SPRING OF 1779, George Washington wrote that "a waggon load of money will scarcely purchase a waggon load of provision."

Gen. Benedict Arnold needed more than one wagonload. While his Saratoga wounds healed, he was serving grandly, expensively, as the commander in Philadelphia. There he had successfully wooed a belle of Tory Philadelphia, Margaret Shippen. For a wedding present, Arnold was giving his Peggy a magnificent country place—Mount Pleasant, a house now open to the public in Philadelphia's Fairmount Park. But some of the wedding bells chimed off key. For one thing, in his letter of proposal Arnold used the selfsame phrases of love and loyalty that he had written a Boston girl six months earlier. ("A form letter!" hooted Kel.) For another, when Arnold gave Peggy beautiful Mount

Pleasant, it was subject to a heavy mortgage, perhaps of several hundred pounds sterling. Thus he became a bridegroom of quicksilver loyalties and generous debt.

"What was a Pennsylvania pound worth in 1779?" asked Josh. I tried to find out, but the value of money was sliding too fast for an easy answer. In January, 1779, a Philadelphia wholesaler sold a barrel of beef for £16, 10s; by December the price was £242, 10s.

But certainly the greatest bargain in 1779 was the $10 that Washington entered as his travel expense in early July — he was studying the land around Stony Point, New York.

Stony Point is a Hudson River peninsula of curiously sculptured shape. It juts like a pier half a mile out into the river, and its irregular knobs of gray rock rise to a height of 150 feet above the water level. Sir Henry Clinton had covered this odd promontory with earthworks, abatis, and a central fort — and had garrisoned his complex with some 600 crack troops. Stony Point seemed as hard as its name.

The neck of the peninsula was so low that tides would cover it. Washington believed a night attack over the neck might take the fortress by surprise. Had the men really learned von Steuben's lessons with the bayonet? The exploit called for picked men

—and a fearless leader. George Washington recalled the British bayonets used in the darkness at Paoli. For Stony Point, he called on the one man most hungering for revenge: Gen. Anthony Wayne.

Late on July 15, the eve of attack, Wayne scribbled a letter dated "near the Hour and Scene of Carnage." He expected to die in this battle, he wrote, and he asked his friend to care for his children. Therewith, Wayne signed his name and fate and joined the midnight march of his 1,200 men.

His two columns moved silently through the marsh, branched out, then moved into the Stony Point defenses. As the surprised

British began to fire, American axemen chopped away the abatis, and special volunteers dashed past the obstructions. Then a whole cataract of men flowed past the barricades and into dark battle. British muskets flashed; men fell—thick—but the Americans used only the bayonet. Inside the second abatis, a bullet struck Wayne. The general's face was covered with blood.

"Carry me up to the fort, boys!" Wayne shouted; men supported each arm, so that he could reel forward, upward, now into the fort itself—*victorious!*

If the drama was bad, Wayne's luck was good: His was only a scalp wound. The news

PAINTING BY F. C. YOHN, CONTINENTAL INSURANCE COMPANY

PAINTING BY FERDINAND DE BRACKELEER, COLLECTION OF HUGH S. WATSON, JR.

Scourge of British commerce, John Paul Jones grips cutlass and pistol before a romanticized version of the Stars and Stripes. The Scottish-born officer served seven years in the patriot cause.

"I have not yet begun to fight!" trumpets Captain Jones from the splintered deck of the Bonhomme Richard. *His immortal words rebuffed the captain of the* Serapis, *who asked if the outgunned Americans had surrendered. Seeing that his only chance for victory lay with muskets and grenades at close quarters, Jones hooked grappling irons to the* Serapis *and lashed a fallen line from the frigate to his own mizzenmast. After two hours* Serapis *struck her colors and the Americans took her captive, leaving their gutted ship to sink.*

147

PAINTING BY FRANK REILLY, CONTINENTAL DISTILLING CORPORATION

Behind the scenes of war, Philadelphia broker Haym Salomon (seated) deposits coin acquired by marketing Continental bills. Superintendent of Finance Robert Morris — in effect, the first Secretary of the Treasury — leans forward at left. By 1780, the government faced financial collapse.

itself excited the young nation, and made Sir Henry Clinton more cautious. The American price was 15 dead and 80 wounded; the British army had lost 20 killed, 74 wounded, 58 missing *and 472 captured.* This record had been carved, von Steuben noted, completely with the bayonet. Yet Anthony Wayne's pen was almost as mighty. His two-sentence report to Washington read: "This fort & Garri-son . . . are our's. Our officers & Men behaved like men who are determined to be free."

Today as we read the old newspaper accounts of Stony Point, we can see more than the news. "The paper looks *blue,*" said Tina.

She was entirely right. Paper-makers were running out of rags and bleaches; by 1779 they had to grind up old printed paper — and add bluing to hide the inky gray.

"I thank you for the Boston Newspapers," Franklin wrote his niece from Paris in 1779. "They perfectly blind me. . . . If you should ever have any Secrets that you wish to be well kept, get them printed in those Papers."

As the American minister plenipotentiary to France, Franklin had secrets aplenty. He was the national agent to wangle French

frank
Reilly

"Hard money" in the form of foreign coins (above) circulated in wartime commerce. But with no power to tax, the Continental Congress found its coffers empty. Like the states, it resorted to printing paper money in abundance. The New Jersey issue (below) and others carried promises of redemption in coin. Inability to back up such notes led to their eventual worthlessness—perpetuated today in a familiar colloquialism, "not worth a Continental."

COINS, SMITHSONIAN INSTITUTION; PAPER CURRENCY, HISTORICAL SOCIETY
OF PENNSYLVANIA; PHOTOGRAPHS BY VICTOR R. BOSWELL, JR.,
NATIONAL GEOGRAPHIC STAFF

gifts and loans. When Virginia sent her adopted spokesman, the brilliant Italian Philip Mazzei, as state agent in Europe, the old sage tactfully kept the national interest supreme. Franklin also worked as a kind of Secretary of the Navy, outfitting ships for a wiry Scot whom the British considered a pirate: one John Paul Jones. Franklin entrusted him with an old armed brigantine and three small warships.

Jones expressed his gratitude to Franklin both in words ("... your ... noble minded instructions would make a coward brave") and also in the name he chose for his flagship, the *Bonhomme Richard,* as "Poor Richard" of Franklin's almanac was called in France.

By September, Jones's raids had spread

panic along the coast of the British Isles. And on the afternoon of September 23, he squinted into his spyglass and saw the Baltic merchant fleet of Britain convoyed by the 50-gun frigate *Serapis* and a sloop of war.

It was after sunset when Jones ordered the firing of a starboard broadside at *Serapis.* "The battle being thus begun," he recalled, "was Continued with Unremitting fury."

One of Jones's midshipmen, Nathaniel Fanning, later wrote, "The wind was now very light ... and the *Serapis* outsailing us by two feet to one.... our men fell in all parts of the ship by scores."

Commodore Jones realized that his only chance was to board and grapple, so he ran his *Richard* onto the stern of *Serapis.* It was

"Give 'em Watts, boys!" shouts the Rev. James Caldwell to Continentals halting a British raid on Springfield, New Jersey, in June, 1780. When they ran short of paper to make wadding for their guns, the "Fighting Parson" burst into a nearby Presbyterian church and scooped up hymnals written by Isaac Watts. Two weeks earlier, a redcoat's bullet had killed the minister's wife.

then that the British captain thought Jones might surrender and called out: "Has your ship struck?"

John Paul Jones's reply was classic: "I have not yet begun to fight!" But begin he now did. He pulled his ship back, maneuvered through a storm of cannonfire, and then caught *Serapis* with grappling irons, attaching his ship firmly—and fatally—in a bow-to-stern embrace. The muzzles of the ships' cannon actually touched. The warriors turned to musket and grenade.

The battle raged in full view of spectators standing on the chalky cliffs of Flamborough Head. Both ships caught fire, and the battle paused while seamen worked as firemen. When the flames died, the battle was renewed by moonlight, the ships clinching and swinging at anchor for about two hours. At last, as his mainmast swayed, the British captain struck his colors, and handed over his sword and his ship.

The heroic *Bonhomme Richard* resembled no victor. Fanning saw "the dead lying in heaps... the blood (American too) over one's shoes." The ship's hull was so shattered that through one gaping hole "one might have drove in with a coach and six." The noble hulk was abandoned and sank.

"The Cruise of our little American Squadron... has had some Success," old Ben Franklin reported proudly to the U.S.A. "... This has put the Enemy to much Expence in marching Troops from Place to Place."

Expense was a growing worry among all the belligerents. Even Queen Marie Antoinette wrote her mother, the Austrian Empress: "We have given up... going to Fontainebleau, on account of the expense of the war.... Our fleet has not met the English..."

But even now d'Estaing was bringing a French fleet and amphibious army from the West Indies for an operation to free Savannah. Joining the French admiral was Count Pulaski's Legion of cavalry and light infantry

marching from Charleston; behind Pulaski came Benjamin Lincoln with larger forces.

About 5,500 allies were drawn up against a garrison of 2,600, so the French and Americans confidently—overconfidently—waited three weeks for a British surrender.

When the allies finally launched their assault on October 9, the Britons had completed their defenses and a South Carolina deserter had revealed the plan of attack. The battle cost a high price in heroes. The same Sergeant Jasper who had won his fame with the flag at Fort Sullivan, carried his regiment's colors—and died there. The dashing Count Pulaski led his cavalry in a charge on the enemy's works and was caught in a fierce crossfire; a canister shot struck him down. He was just one of the 244 allies to perish in

this, the bloodiest battle since Bunker Hill.

Lincoln wanted to continue the Savannah siege, but Count d'Estaing did not; the French fleet again sailed away, discouraging patriots, heartening southern Tories, and causing the Londoners—when they learned of it—to fire joyous salutes in St. James's Park.

At the French court in Marly, however, because the autumn was rainy and spirits were low, the royal retinue returned to a diversion temporarily banned: gambling. In one night, His Majesty lost almost half his private income for a month, an ambassador reported on November 17, 1779.

"I wonder what Washington was doing at the same time," said Kel. I checked Washington's collected letters and found that the General had done much paper work at his West Point headquarters. In one note he wrote of the "scantiness of our supplies in the way of clothing." In another he settled "a command this winter with the main army in the neighbourhood of Morristown."

That winter in Morristown, New Jersey, was the worst of the war. A clear-eyed veteran of Valley Forge, Baron von Steuben said that the New York Brigade "exhibited the most shocking picture of misery I have ever seen, scarce a man having wherewithal to cover his nakedness. . . ."

Before December was over, Washington begged help from the governors with the warning, "there is every appearance that the Army will infallibly disband in a fortnight." But somehow he held things together.

The first week of 1780 saw snowdrifts four

151

feet high. This was the winter the Hudson froze solid enough for travelers to cross its ice at King's Ferry. And farther south, the British in New York supplied Staten Island by sleigh. Eight inches of snow still lay on the ground in March. Hand to mouth, the army subsisted. On April 12, Washington noted not "one ounce of Meat fresh or salt in the Magazine." On the 14th bread was the only food.

While waiting for food to arrive, Washington received a newspaper from New York—the *Gazette* published by the Tory Rivington. It brought news of a major disaster: After a hard siege, the British had at last taken Charleston, South Carolina, on May 12.

The date seemed, and still seems, ironic. In the springtime, when we visited Charleston, the city resembled a pageant more than a battlefield: neat, solid homes of handmade brick . . . an ocean breeze scented with salt . . . and a whole spectrum of garden flowers—and nowhere a hint of war. Yet in the park

beside our hotel, we could see a fragment of Gen. Benjamin Lincoln's defense wall.

This great and graceful city had resisted Sir Henry Clinton and Lord Cornwallis for 45 long days. But after a walpurgis night of bombardment—"it appeared as if the stars were tumbling down," said Moultrie—to spare civilians, the patriots surrendered. Cornwallis insisted on a strange, painful point: The vanquished army of 5,500 could not march out, colors flying, to the tune of a British march. Militia could not march at all. So the Stars and Stripes were ordered cased; nearly 1,600 Continentals stepped to "the Turk's march"—and remembered.

Like Cornwallis before us, we traveled northwest from Charleston toward Camden, South Carolina. As we drove, I handed Kel a road map and the assignment "to find us that battlefield." We missed it completely, turned around, tried again. But at the highway fork where some historic marker should

ENGRAVING FROM "BATTLES OF THE UNITED STATES BY SEA AND LAND," BY HENRY B. DAWSON; AND ROWLAND SCHERMAN

THE MILES BREWTON HOUSE

Scratched on marble, probably by a British officer, a profile of Sir Henry Clinton marks a mantel in a Charleston home, his South Carolina headquarters in 1780. St. Michael's steeple sheltered patriot lookouts till the town fell on May 12, in one of the worst American defeats of the war. At the start of the siege, the British set up cannon about a half-mile from town defenses.

have stood, we could find only a stand of clean-smelling young pines.

"Maybe they moved it for the road repairs," Kel suggested. Maybe. But there was a certain poetry in this omission: For since the Battle of Camden most of his compatriots have passed by Gen. Horatio Gates.

Gates, commanding the patriot forces for the whole South, simply employed the same boldness that some men thought he lacked. His hungry troops, however, had foraged on green corn, and thus were weakened by illness. On a hot night's march, the Americans collided with Cornwallis's army. Gates ordered a bold assault in the dawn's first

Nobleman and fighting man, Charles, General Lord Cornwallis, led an army in America though opposed to British policies that had led to war. His decisive defeat of the overbold Horatio Gates at Camden, South Carolina, on August 16, 1780, caused the Congress to look for a new general.

Baring powdered hair in a grave salute, Gen. Nathanael Greene greets his unfortunate colleague Gates at Charlotte, North Carolina. Assuming command of the Southern Department on December 3, 1780, Greene built up its army from remnants left by Camden. He lost battle after battle but won his southern campaigns. His great foe Cornwallis, who could never outwit him, called Greene "as dangerous as Washington."

light. Ill-conceived and undirected, the attack only prodded the British to charge with bayonets—and to win.

General Gates was soon far away. As his men fled, a fine race horse carried him to Charlotte, 70 miles distant, in a single day's ride—and out of battle forever.

Humiliating as Camden was, America felt a new and deeper shock just one month later. On September 23, a somewhat scruffy young civilian was detained near Tarrytown, New York, by three American militiamen. In his boot the man carried papers "of a very dangerous tendency," as a report soon noted. And, indeed, the papers were a military inventory of all West Point and a pass signed by Gen. Benedict Arnold, by now the commanding officer of West Point.

The prisoner was Maj. John André, dashing party-planner in Philadelphia and now in charge of espionage for Sir Henry Clinton. André's mistake was that he had conferred with his accomplice Benedict Arnold and put on civilian clothes within American lines.

"But why was West Point so important?" Josh asked me. "Because of the army school?" I explained that the Academy came later. But the Hudson River scenery makes its own explanation of strategy. West Point overlooks a sharp 90-degree turn in the river channel; sea-going ships must slow down here and ride within easy gun-range of the shore. A battery of cannon here—and a massive chain stretched across the river—controlled all Hudson valley commerce. And the Hudson, of course, cut the United States in two. Was West Point really the key to the continent? Obviously, General Arnold

"Great Chain" that spanned the Hudson spans the years for a young visitor to West Point, New York. Americans stretched 1,000 links — 60 tons — across the river in April, 1778, to block British warships. The Point dominates the west bank of the river (lithograph above), where Fort Clinton stands atop the bluff. Constitution Island shapes the channel into a hairpin bend. French artist Pierre Charles L'Enfant, who later planned Washington, D. C., made the original watercolor about 1780 — the year Benedict Arnold took command at the Point. Cadets at the U. S. Military Academy crowd the walls of old Fort Putnam (right) during a military arts lecture. An instructor explains how the hillside bastion protected Fort Arnold about half a mile below.

156

thought it worth his whole American career.)

But why did Arnold commit treason? For two centuries his life has puzzled scholars, poets, and moralists. We can only guess, and measure what evidence we have: the 16 months that he dickered with the British... the rank and pay and pensions that he would hold in His Majesty's service... the sum of £6,315 in hard sterling.

Could the answer be as simple as greed? After all, men have defected for as little as thirty pieces of silver.

If Arnold's motives were low, at least the drama was high—and broadly acted against the operatic backdrop of the New York Highlands. Arnold was eating breakfast—and expecting George Washington to arrive momentarily—when he learned of André's capture. He went upstairs to take leave of

Caught with Benedict Arnold's plans of West Point in his boot, British Maj. John André submits to a search by militiamen near Tarrytown, New York. Condemned as a spy, André turns sharply at the sight of a gallows — learning only then that he would not die, as he pleaded, by a firing squad. Congress gave each of his three captors a silver medal.

Peggy, and hurried to his barge to join the British sloop *Vulture* downstream.

Washington arrived, waited awhile for Arnold, then received the André papers. While Peggy Arnold feigned madness in her room, the fantastic news spread wide. America had lost a hero and saved West Point.

One officer who had served with Arnold wrote these dark, searching words: "Treason! Treason! Treason! black as hell! . . . we were all astonishment, each peeping at his next neighbor to see if any treason was hanging about him. Nay, we even descended to a critical examination of ourselves."

So at West Point the name of Fort Arnold was abruptly dropped. And on British-occupied Long Island, patriot spies momentarily lay low. A Yale classmate of Nathan Hale, Benjamin Tallmadge, had organized

a ring that even today seems sophisticated. The patriots used aliases ("Culper, Sr. and Jr."), codes, invisible ink, and if not cloaks-and-daggers at least petticoats, for messages were signaled by a petticoat on a clothesline.

Soon after André's execution as a spy, Tallmadge himself went spying on the British. He had a "scheme of annoying the enemy," as he put it. The British were gathering their supplies for another New York winter, and tightening their hold on Long Island. Tallmadge proposed a raid to destroy "a large quantity of hay and forage . . . at Corum. . . ."

Tallmadge and some "100 selected men" left the Connecticut beaches in whaleboats and crossed Long Island Sound. At Fort St. George, "the sentinel . . . demanded, 'Who comes there?' and fired. Before the smoke from his gun had cleared his vision, my

sergeant . . . reached him with his bayonet, and prostrated him." That sergeant, one Elijah Churchill, Major Tallmadge, and about 10 others proceeded to Coram, burned 300 tons of royal hay, and returned "without the loss of a man," Tallmadge proudly noted.

The operation brought an even greater cause for pride: Under the orders of General Washington the brave Sergeant Churchill was presented the Purple Heart—the first decoration in modern times honoring a non-commissioned warrior.

Other spies and raiders were working in Appalachia. Lord Cornwallis invaded North Carolina and brushed aside the militia who tried to stop him. But in the steep, hard backwoods of the Carolinas and what is now Tennessee, the "over-mountain men" took up their rifles in the rebel cause.

The serious, very professional Maj. Patrick Ferguson, commanding about 1,000 Tories near the Blue Ridge, tried to scare the backwoodsmen. He set free a prisoner and sent a message by him, ordering them to disband or "he would march his army over the mountains, hang their leaders and lay their country waste with fire and sword."

The challenge was a blunder. Now the ruggedly independent mountain men gathered at present-day Elizabethton, Tennessee, and joined other volunteers at Quaker Meadows, the home of the McDowell brothers.

"Whose home?" demanded 10-year-old Josh. I showed him the names of Col. Charles and Maj. Joseph McDowell, and Josh—whose full name is Joseph Shea McDowell—exulted: "I guess we were finally on the right side!"

Ours was even a winning side. The hardy Americans vengefully pursued the Bulldog, as Ferguson was called. He chose to stop on a lonely, forested hill and wrote to Cornwallis, "I arrived today at Kings Mountain & have taken a post where I do not think I can be forced...." Once again Major Ferguson was wrong. By horseback, more Americans converged at an open place used for cattle roundups and called the Cowpens. Then, on the men rode to Kings Mountain.

We followed our tough, distant relatives to visit the national military park at that same strange formation: the freakishly steep, 60-foot peak jutting starkly up from gentle farmlands. Ferguson had chosen a classic, castle-like high point to defend—but the trees below offered superb protection for mountaineer riflemen.

All night the patriots rode their horses to get here; then they dismounted to fight. The battle began about 3 p.m. when the Tories noticed rebels below them. To keep the enemy from surrounding the ridge, Ferguson attacked with both bayonet charges and volleys from the British muskets. The mountain men just stepped behind trees and took deadly aim with their long rifles.

Hard-pressed, Ferguson blew a high, piercing note on his silver whistle, and then astride his horse led a charge to break out of the deadly circle. A rifle bullet struck him. And as Ferguson was falling from his horse, seven more bullets hit his dying body.

"Real marksmanship," marvelled Kel, "and a real irony!" He lifted a rifle from the park collection and inspected the action. This was Patrick Ferguson's own invention—patented

in December, 1776—a breech-loading rifle that could have added tremendous fire power, had the British adopted it. Instead, they kept the Brown Bess musket. Ferguson died by the muzzle-loaded rifles of his American enemies. His body rests in Kings Mountain near a giant poplar that may have survived the same strange battle. His Majesty's loss here was singular: Every loyalist in the fight was killed, wounded, or captured—about 1,000. The patriots lost but 28 killed.

But more than that, Kings Mountain startled Cornwallis. Concerned for his own safety, he retreated southward. Lord Cornwallis could not know how swiftly the rebel volunteers vanished homeward.

In history, this one-battle American army stands as isolated as that strange mountain rising from Carolina farmland. Yet the over-mountain men got more than vengeance: They bought America time. While Cornwallis waited briefly on the defensive, patriots feverishly rebuilt their army. Perhaps they would have time enough to save the South.

Guns blazing, modern sharpshooters fire from covering woods, recalling the Battle of Kings Mountain, South Carolina, in 1780. Ordered to "shout like hell and fight like devils," patriots turned back three waves of loyalists. As the Tories' leader, Maj. Patrick Ferguson, tried to break the rebel lines, back-country marksmen shot him from the saddle; he died as he fell.

With final victory in sight, Washington and French commander Count de Rochambeau (pointing), plan

1781: "The World Turned Upside Down"

PAINTING BY LOUIS-CHARLES AUGUSTE COUDER, MUSÉE DE VERSAILLES

The storming of British redoubts during the allies' siege of Yorktown, the last major campaign of the war.

WE FIRST SAW the Waxhaw Creek country by late afternoon light. Kel cast an observant eye over the clay hills and said, "Those banks actually look blood red."

The comment seemed symbolic. For here, along the line that separates North and South Carolina, was born the ugly and undying legend of Bloody Tarleton and the Continental byword "Tarleton's quarter." Near this spot Banastre Tarleton—a dashing cavalryman, red of hair and black of fame—won skirmishes and infamy. His men bayoneted 113 Americans to death and wounded nearly 200 others—even after they called for quarter and showed a flag of truce.

As 1780 ended, patriots could see their problems in a variety of shapes. In Richmond, Governor Thomas Jefferson gave an Indian servant a tip of £5, 10s, on New Year's Eve; his generosity sounds larger than life, since a Virginia pound was then worth only one *seventy-fifth* of an English pound—about threepence. Financially, America was awash in a dangerous tide of paper.

On the first evening of 1781, some 1,500 soldiers of the Pennsylvania Line mutinied at

163

Brave and defiant, 13-year-old Andrew Jackson deflects a blow from a British officer's saber. Arrested in a cousin's home as one of the Waxhaw Whigs —a group of bushwhacking patriots—and ordered to clean the mud from the officer's boots, the boy angrily refused. Slashed across his hand and scalp, he bore the scars for life. Marched 40 miles to a prison camp, he regained his freedom a few days later in an exchange of captives. Jackson went on to face the British again in the War of 1812, and became the seventh President of the United States.

British cavalryman Banastre Tarleton (below), earning his nickname "Bloody Tarleton," slaughters cornered Virginia Continentals at the Waxhaws, South Carolina, in May, 1780. Disregarding a flag of truce, the British bayoneted to death 113 Americans.

Morristown. The men respectfully resisted the eloquence of General Wayne, marched off, and seized Princeton. Tense negotiations took more than a week, and grievances like back pay and enlistment dates took longer to settle. The mutiny came to an end, but it left a question for American commanders. How long would men serve a government that could not pay or supply them?

In December Gen. Nathanael Greene had relieved General Gates in Charlotte, North Carolina, taking command of 1,482 troops listed as "fit and ready." Their appearance, Greene noted, "was wretched beyond description." Greene set to work.

Just as Washington had picked Greene at Valley Forge, so Greene picked an able warrior, Col. William R. Davie, to act as commissary general. Davie protested: He knew nothing about accounting for funds. Don't worry, Greene assured him, they had no funds to keep and no prospect of getting any.

Soon Greene had other help: Von Steuben was recruiting troops in Richmond. The brilliant Henry Lee, "Light-Horse Harry," would handle special guerrilla assignments. And finally the arthritic Daniel Morgan had returned as a brigadier general from an aching, year-long retirement in Virginia. He would command a small corps of light infantry, militiamen, and light cavalry under Lt. Col. William Washington, a cousin of the Commander-in-Chief. Greene cautioned the Old Wagoner about the "useless militia."

Then, in the face of Cornwallis's 3,200 men, Greene divided the American forces. Morgan would proceed west "to give protection ... and spirit up the people...."

Greene had his reasons. Both parts of his army could more easily eat off the land, and each part could move swiftly—to harass the British or to retreat.

During the first week of 1781 Morgan's men struck the post of Ninety Six in western

165

(B)

(D)

At the Cowpens on January 17, Ban Tarleton and his green-clad British dragoons ride
north to defeat. His supply train (A) stops
as the battle opens. By Dan Morgan's orders,
two skirmish lines of patriot militia fire and
fall back; they withdraw to the rear (B),
slipping past the main line of Continentals.
When Tarleton charges confidently, that
line holds; he sends Highlanders to the
left (C) to outflank it. As the patriots
move back, he thinks the battle won. Suddenly, at Morgan's command, the Continentals counterattack. William Washington's
cavalry (D) smash the British right;
mounted militia (E) strike the left and
the skirmishers rejoin the fight in the same
area. Enveloped on both flanks and hit
hard in front, the British scatter and flee
in confusion. Tarleton (F) tries in vain to
rally his troopers. He fled at a gallop with
Colonel Washington at his heels. In the
shadow of the South Carolina Blue Ridge,
Morgan had scored a brilliant victory.

PAINTED FOR NATIONAL GEOGRAPHIC BY RICHARD SCHLECHT

Richard Schlecht

South Carolina, killing 150 loyalists and taking 40 prisoners.

Morgan waited for Cornwallis to retaliate. The move came promptly. If Greene could split his forces in two, the British would raise the ante: Cornwallis divided his forces into *three* groups, one to hold Camden, one with himself, and the third—under the terrible Bloody Tarleton—to find Morgan and, declared the orders, "push him to the utmost."

Push him Ban Tarleton did—to the Cowpens, that rolling plain famous for roundups. And so developed a classic struggle between villainy and virtue.

Tarleton followed Morgan "like a bloodhound," said the Old Wagoner. "I did not intend to fight that day . . . but as matters were circumstanced, no time was to be lost." With the Broad River cutting off an American retreat and with open woods permitting easy entry for Tarleton's horsemen, the Cowpens looked like King George's terrain. But Morgan deployed his men brilliantly and understood them perfectly.

Some Americans have left us their recollections of Morgan's night before the battle. "I don't believe he slept a wink," wrote one of the cavalrymen, Thomas Young. "He went among the volunteers, helped them fix their swords, joked with them about their sweethearts, told them to keep in good spirits, and the day would be ours." Everything depended on the staying power of the militia, and each militiaman knew just what was expected of him: only two shots. Then he could retreat in good order. With the confident

Morgan in charge, every man felt secure.

When we visited the Cowpens Battlefield, Congress was still debating whether to buy this land. The National Park Service owned only a lot-sized plot that nestled among orchards, cotton fields, clumps of pine, and some historic pasture with grazing Herefords.

The park plot includes the slope where Morgan himself watched the battle; we could enjoy, I announced, the general's own view.

"Not really," said Kel, who likes finding a hole in his father's information. "Morgan was on horseback." Kel hopped up on the fender of our car to add altitude. "He could see more from up here." Kel was not just quibbling: On the bitterly cold morning of January 17, 1781, that horse-high elevation gave the patriots a most important advantage. As Tarleton approached he could be seen—but could not himself see beyond that gentle slope. That rise hid Tarleton's comeuppance.

The British set out for battle at 3 a.m., but Morgan's men still took time to eat a solid

Stately mansion built for Governor William Tryon in 1770 stands beside the Trent River in North Carolina. The "Palace" symbolized the luxuries that turned many poor hill-country taxpayers against the royal cause. Among those patriots lived Nancy Hart (below), Georgia's legendary "war woman," six feet tall. When six Tories raided her cabin, she reputedly shot one dead, wounded another, and held the rest at musket point until her husband returned to help hang them.

Near Guilford Courthouse, North Carolina, the 1st Maryland charges British Guards. At the end of the battle on March 15, Cornwallis held the field—one-fourth of his army casualties. Peter Francisco, a giant among patriots, claimed 11 redcoats with his 5-foot sword; below, at Ward's Tavern in Virginia later in 1781, he stands off nine dragoons single-handed.

breakfast before the brightly clad enemy appeared—"right there, behind that peach orchard," as Kel read the map.

First Tarleton met a line of riflemen. He pushed them back—but into a second line. The Americans fired with effect, but Tarleton was confident he could scatter them. He charged again. The militia fired and then fell back, confirming Tarleton's contempt—but actually obeying old Dan Morgan to the letter. British regulars pushed again, with reserves brought up. The main line of Continentals stood firm and fought hard.

Then, when Tarleton's flanking movement seemed to be working, brilliant plans gave way to the laws of chance. Over the noise of guns, the Virginians misunderstood a command; instead of turning to face the British, the Americans retreated slightly in good order. The overconfident Tarleton misread this retreat as American panic.

Sure of victory, he encouraged his men in a pell-mell charge. The confused, disorderly British now swept over that horse-high ridge head-on into stubborn, brave, well-ordered Americans. While his random chargers bumped against this wall, Tarleton found still another surprise: Colonel Washington's horsemen smashed his flank and rear, and the Continentals rushed forward with flashing bayonets. The militia—the same men Tarleton thought he had scared away—reappeared and opened a deadly fire. Slammed on all sides, the British faltered, broke, and fled.

Only a few made good their escape, but these included Bloody Banastre Tarleton himself. Behind him, he left some 900 British killed, wounded, or captured—about nine-tenths of his whole force.

Only 12 Americans died at the Cowpens. By good planning, good luck, and good insight into the nature of his men, old Dan Morgan had indeed spirited up the people. Now Greene could unite his forces and conduct a kind of magician's quick-handed campaign—one that led directly to Yorktown. A saucy verse soon described the strategy to the tune of "Yankee Doodle":

> *Cornwallis led a country dance,*
> *The like was never seen, sir,*
> *Much retrograde and much advance,*
> *And all with General Greene, sir.*

Greene quick-stepped north to the Dan River, and Cornwallis—confident that Greene had too few boats to cross it—followed close at his heels. But clever Nathanael Greene had prepared for this very movement long in advance by gathering all the boats for miles; he slipped across on St. Valentine's Day, leaving Lord Cornwallis high and dry. His Lordship could do little now but dance a retrograde in his turn—back into North Carolina.

In a letter to Dan Morgan, Greene had phrased his southern strategy: "Put nothing to the hazard, a retreat may be disagreeable but not disgraceful. Regard not the opinion of the day."

In other quarters the opinion of the day ranked high. Tidewater Virginia was feeling the venom of Benedict Arnold's new loyalties; but his raids were well chaperoned by other British officers who never quite trusted this turncoat-redcoat. Some places he burned, but Berkeley, the Harrison family's big plantation on the James River, Arnold merely looted. (When we visited this proud old manor house, Josh began to realize the nature of

such raids. With the bitterness of a personal betrayal he said, "Arnold was a real nut!")

Other disagreeable tasks faced the Continental Congress in Philadelphia. Without the help of a court system or a well-organized executive branch, the delegates functioned as the whole national government.

John Adams had summarized Congressional work: "When 50 or 60 Men have a Constitution to form for a great Empire, at the same Time that they have a Country of fifteen hundred Miles extent to fortify, Millions to arm and train, a Naval Power to begin, an extensive Commerce to regulate, numerous Tribes of Indians to negotiate with, a standing Army of Twenty seven Thousand Men to raise, pay, victual and officer, I really shall pity those 50 or 60 Men."

By early 1781, the 50 or 60 men were waging a war almost worldwide. High-handed British seizure of merchant ships had alienated the League of Armed Neutrality—Russia, Denmark, Sweden, and the Netherlands. Great Britain had declared war on the Dutch in December, 1780. Spain, the Bourbon ally of France, was contributing money directly to

171

Meager fare of baked potatoes offered by Gen. Francis Marion startles a British officer on a prisoner-exchange mission. His hosts' self-sacrifice reportedly so moved him that he quit the army. Guerrilla raids from South Carolina swampland (below) gave Marion the name "Swamp Fox."

the U.S.A. And through all these events, Congress exchanged diplomats, reviewed courts martial, borrowed money—and still lacked the power to levy a single tax.

By 1781, Continental currency had purchased the enduring cliché, "not worth a Continental." Merchants refused it. At least once the United States Board of Treasury was actually threatened with eviction for non-payment of its Philadelphia rent.

New York's Tory publisher James Rivington exulted, "The Congress is finally bankrupt! Last Saturday a large body of the inhabitants with paper dollars in their hats by way of cockades, paraded the streets of Philadelphia... with a *DOG TARRED,* and instead of ...feathers, his back was covered with the Congress' paper dollars."

Desperately, the Congress turned to Robert Morris, a Philadelphia merchant-banker-shipowner who had served as a gifted member of the Congress. Morris was unanimously elected superintendent of finance.

"The least breach of faith must ruin us forever," he said. "The United States may command everything I have, except my integrity...." Thus Morris began to prop up American credit with his own personal signature and the private guarantees of his friends, prosperous merchants.

General Washington sighed with relief but wrote, "I do not suppose that by Art magick, he can do more than recover us, by degrees from the labyrinth into which our finance is plunged."

Washington's stepson Jack Custis felt uneasy about his £48,000 mortgage on the Arlington estate; Jack had borrowed good money, and now he wanted to treat his lenders squarely by writing a new contract. The general found Jack's proposals "fair and equitable" for "the money is in fact worth little or

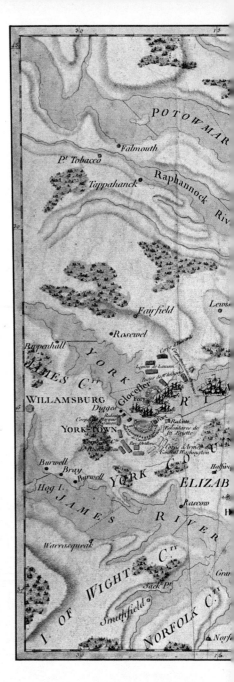

French battle plan from the 18th century illustrates the siege of Yorktown and naval action off the Virginia capes, in the fall of 1781. While the French fleet of the Count de Grasse blocked Admiral Thomas Graves's British reinforcements from reaching Cornwallis, Washington and Rochambeau bombarded Yorktown. On September 5, the English squadron sparred with De Grasse, then withdrew to New York. Six weeks later Cornwallis surrendered.

nothing." Such was the need for fiscal reform.

Robert Morris got some needed help from the gifted Jewish immigrant Haym Salomon. Though thrown into New York's Provost prison — often a sentence of death — Salomon had soon eased himself out by serving as a translator for the British and the Hessians. Salomon did not stop with translations; he also urged the German soldiers to desert.

In 1778 Salomon himself, rounded up and sentenced to hang for spying, managed to desert New York for Philadelphia. With the help of friends, he opened a securities business; by 1781 he was able to find buyers for Morris's paper currency and to provide coin for the government's war chest. Salomon also lent generous sums of his own money, interest free, to delegates in Congress, among them James Madison, when their states could not pay their expenses.

For all its difficulties, the country had at least adopted a constitution. Congress had drafted, and the states had approved, the Articles of Confederation by March, 1781. Church bells and guns saluted the event. "Thus America," commented the *Pennsylvania Packet*, "... is growing up in war into greatness...."

So were individuals. The prodigy Henry Lee, graduated at 17 from the college at Princeton and now a heroic young lieutenant colonel, was carving a new reputation in the South. General Greene had assigned the patrician Lee to work closely with Francis Marion. This strange team, Light-Horse Harry and the Swamp Fox, proved an inspired combination. Lee's Legion, dazzlingly plumed, could move swiftly to support those muddy men who followed the lean and swarthy Marion.

This was true guerrilla war: hit-and-run operations to wound a powerful enemy — and to vanish before he could react. American regulars and irregulars cooperated smoothly.

What with the raids of Col. Andrew Pickens — "the Gamecock" — and the magnetic Col. Thomas Sumter, the moss-draped forests of South Carolina soon became sinister and uncertain for the British.

Cornwallis himself was still searching for that Utopian spot where the loyalists would help. "I erected the King's Standard," he wrote, "and invited ... all loyal subjects to repair to it...." But such repairs were rare. Soon his Lordship sadly reported that the Tories' "friendship was only passive."

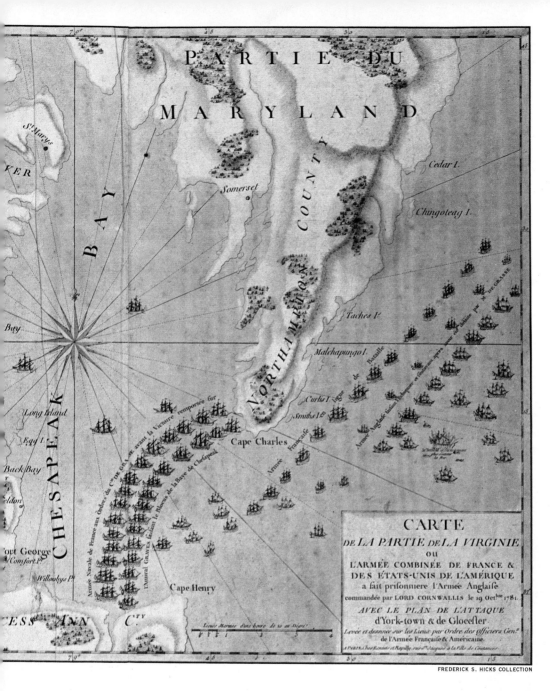

While the British army waned, Greene's waxed. Reinforcements arrived from Virginia. And though most of his 4,500 men were untested militia—less than one-fourth veterans of any combat—Greene still felt strong enough to stand his ground at Guilford Courthouse, North Carolina.

That ground was uneven: scrabble farmland scored by a deep ravine and tangled woods. Across it, Greene disposed his troops in three lines like Morgan's at Cowpens—but with much more distance between them.

Greatly outnumbered, Lord Cornwallis brought up some 2,000 troops about midday on a clear March 15. He pushed against the first of Greene's three lines. It gave way. The second line held longer, but again the militia scattered. Now the third American line came up for test; crack Continentals, they held firm. The 1st Maryland even counterattacked. Cornwallis himself entered the fray, borrowing a dragoon's horse when his own was shot, and bravely rallying his veterans. Finally, as the battle stood in doubt, Cornwallis gave

175

the cruel, essential order for his artillery to fire grapeshot at the Continentals—and at his own men fighting at close quarters. The patriots reeled backward.

With one more try—a new cavalry charge perhaps—Greene might have won the day. Or lost his army. He avoided the risk, let well enough alone, and eased away from the field of battle, which Cornwallis enjoyed as the victor's symbolic campsite. But of his 2,000 troops, Cornwallis had lost 532 killed, wounded, or missing—and with them, his power to take the offensive.

General Sir Henry Clinton commented grimly that Cornwallis's action at Guilford Courthouse and afterward caused "the ruin of a fine army and the ultimate loss of an opulent and important province."

But Cornwallis believed that "Until Virginia is in a manner subdued, our hold of the Carolinas must be difficult if not precarious." So, with his 1,500 survivors, Cornwallis moved to the Old Dominion, leaving the able young Lord Rawdon with a precarious hold in the Carolinas.

Greene let Cornwallis go, then set about freeing South Carolina and Georgia. Marion's swamp fighters joined Harry Lee's horsemen to grab outposts like Fort Watson with its 120 royalist defenders—a lonely small stockade on an ancient Indian mound.

Now Greene gathered his forces upon a field with uncomfortable memories: He would try to retake Camden, Britain's strongest point outside Charleston.

We could understand Greene's spirit when we visited the site, for like Greene, we came in the surging month of April. Plums and dogwood were in full flower. He must have felt as optimistic as the season. But Lord Rawdon had already heard of Greene's approach. Instead of waiting for a siege, he hastily prepared an army for the offensive, arming every man he could find, even musicians and drummers. ("You mean *drummer boys?*" asked Rob in some shock. "They tried to shoot *us* Americans?")

They did not merely try. Rawdon's force surprised General Greene while he sipped his breakfast coffee on Hobkirk's Hill. The battle was hard, but the British drove Greene off. Again he had exacted a high price for real estate. Discouraged but determined, Greene wrote the story of his campaign: "We fight, get beat, rise and fight again."

While Greene lay low near Camden, Lee's Legion thundered south through hackberry thickets to meet Francis Marion's guerrillas and take Fort Motte, a fine plantation house where the British were entrenched.

Now Rebecca Motte encouraged Marion and Lee to burn her home if necessary to get the British out. With "a smile of complacency" she furnished the fire arrows to ignite the roof. The 150 British surrendered, the patriots put out the fire, and Mrs. Motte entertained both the British officers and their captors at her own dinner table. Henry Lee was amazed at her "ease, vivacity, and good sense,"

By candlelight, Washington checks a map on the night before battle, routine in his siege of Cornwallis at Yorktown. The Commander-in-Chief used the tent of unbleached linen (left) for his headquarters during the last stages of the war.

qualities that my daughter Tina also admired in "a lady who didn't lose her cool." The British soon pulled back all the way to Charleston.

As the spring of 1781 turned to summer, eyes moved toward Virginia, where Lafayette—"not strong enough even to get beaten," as he joked—was playing tag with Cornwallis.

Washington was both worried and apologetic when he wrote Thomas Jefferson in the first week of June: "The progress which the enemy are making in Virginia is very alarming. . . ." In a letter he dared only hint at his plans for the British—but "should we, by a lucky coincidence . . . gain a Naval superiority their ruin would be inevitable."

Jefferson needed encouragement. That very week Tarleton's horsemen came within minutes of capturing Governor Jefferson himself at Monticello.

But even now, Washington's "lucky coincidence" was moving upon the seas. Admiral de Grasse was bringing a large French fleet first to the West Indies and then to Chesapeake Bay and the Virginia coast—some 3,000 troops. The French urged an attack upon Cornwallis, and Washington agreed.

In mid-August he began to organize a large-scale movement of troops: 2,000 Continentals and nearly 5,000 French regulars would march some 450 miles south to Virginia—and in secrecy, to hide the strategy from Clinton in New York.

It worked. Clinton feared an attack on New York until September 2, when he finally suspected Washington's destination. By then, a parade two miles long had already moved through the gritty streets of Philadelphia, stirring "a dust like a smothering snow," as one chronicler reported.

Yet that very night, in a letter to Lafayette, Washington confided his "impatience and anxiety" to know "what is become of the Count de Grasse" and his French fleet. Everything depended on timing—immediate victory or ruin. Even now the Count de Rochambeau was lending $20,000 in specie from his own war chest to pay the restless patriot troops.

With the omniscience of history, we can see what Washington could not: Just two days later, De Grasse would put 3,000 French troops ashore on Virginia's historic Jamestown Island. They joined Lafayette, Wayne, and von Steuben—those great sentinels who would now keep Cornwallis surrounded in a tiny tobacco port on the River York. Nor was

that all. The 24 great French ships, with 1,700 guns and 19,000 seamen, ran off a weaker British fleet. Cornwallis was now blockaded by land and sea. But he might still break out; as Greene said, His Lordship still had "great pride and great obstinacy."

Greene himself in the same September week was fighting a large battle—the last pitched battle, we know now, that Americans would fight in this war. Greene came upon the British at Eutaw Springs, on the road to Charleston, South Carolina.

Today much of the battlefield is drowned by a system of lakes, but we found that the banks still conserved the forested, mossy mood of that historic September 8. Greene's 2,400 men first surprised and captured 100 British foragers who were gathering sweet potatoes. The king's 2,000 troops—many of them loyalists—then formed for battle beside Eutaw Creek.

On the hot, muggy September day, the armies fought for three desperate, closely disputed hours. In a sense, the Americans were defeated by their own poverty; hungry and thirsty Continentals stopped to forage in the British camp. Greene suffered nearly 500 casualties in the confusion, and was again pushed from the field. The British counted 436 killed and wounded—and 400 men taken prisoner. The injured redcoats crept off to the refuge of Charleston.

And in this hard way, strong, wise Nathanael Greene won his whole southern campaign without once winning a battle. Now his task changed: He must somehow hold together his impoverished, mutinous army until Washington could bring down the British.

We followed Washington's march toward Yorktown as the Virginian entertained his comrades-in-arms at Mount Vernon. This was Washington's first wartime visit to his beloved home overlooking the Potomac, and he offered his guests "hospitality and princely

In a furious onslaught against redcoat defenders, patriot troops storm a redoubt protecting the British garrison at Yorktown on October 14. By bayonet alone, the Americans took the stronghold; their commander, young Lt. Col. Alexander Hamilton, had ordered his men to charge with their guns unloaded. With a simultaneous French attack, the assault weakened the British lines and hastened Yorktown's surrender five days later.

HOWARD PYLE, WILMINGTON SOCIETY OF THE FINE ARTS, DELAWARE ART CENTER

Guns in the blue paint of French ordnance mark their old lines at Yorktown. The mortar fired explosives; cannon pounded earthworks.

Like the British drummer boy who climbed a parapet and beat the call to parley in 1781, a youngster climbs the earthworks tracing the French line at Yorktown. In brilliant 18th-century costume, he visited the battlefield during ceremonies on the anniversary of Cornwallis's surrender.

entertainment," as Jonathan Trumbull wrote.

Again, history's perspective gives us a galling irony. In the same week that Washington reached Mount Vernon, Benedict Arnold made another sort of homecoming to his own Connecticut — with brutal raids on New London and Groton. Arnold's prisoners were butchered and New London burned; and this neurotic, sordid gesture on September 6, 1781, was the last engagement between patriots and royal troops in the north.

As the allies marched south, we followed them, consulting modern highway maps and a scholar's old chart: Washington traveled much the same trail that he had used as a Burgess headed for Williamsburg. Country roads still stitch the crooked tidewater route: Dumfries, Fredericksburg, Bowling Green, Aylett. We admired the Mattaponi River — big, slow, shaded dark by great trees.

In a few hours we made the same trip that took Washington four days.

The general made his headquarters in the familiar surroundings of Williamsburg. He wrote Greene: "Our Operations are fast drawing to a Point of Commencement . . . I hope to open Trenches upon the Enemy's Works. . . . The Enemy are not idle on their Part. Lord Cornwallis has collected his troops on York River, and taken two posts. One in York, the other in Gloucester [on the opposite bank] to defend himself against our Siege. . . ."

At close range today we can examine cannon and redoubts and the line of trenches. Yet Yorktown seems more like a pageant than a deadly battle. This was a stylized

Cattle graze in Surrender Field, where British soldiers laid down their arms on a sunny

October 19, 1781. The McDowells, accompanied by a ranger, tour the national historical park.

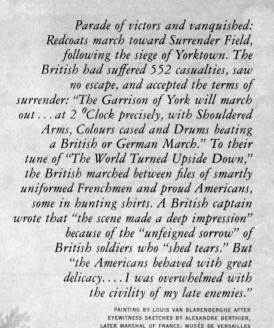

Parade of victors and vanquished: Redcoats march toward Surrender Field, following the siege of Yorktown. The British had suffered 552 casualties, saw no escape, and accepted the terms of surrender: "The Garrison of York will march out ... at 2 ⁰Clock precisely, with Shouldered Arms, Colours cased and Drums beating a British or German March." To their tune of "The World Turned Upside Down," the British marched between files of smartly uniformed Frenchmen and proud Americans, some in hunting shirts. A British captain wrote that "the scene made a deep impression" because of the "unfeigned sorrow" of British soldiers who "shed tears." But "the Americans behaved with great delicacy.... I was overwhelmed with the civility of my late enemies."

PAINTING BY LOUIS VAN BLARENBERGHE AFTER EYEWITNESS SKETCHES BY ALEXANDRE BERTHIER, LATER MARSHAL OF FRANCE; MUSÉE DE VERSAILLES

artillery siege. Its art lay in an orchestration of ships, horses, cannon, and men from two continents—all coming together at precisely the right moment.

The siege began on September 28, when some 8,845 Americans joined nearly 8,000 French troops in a ring around the little port and Cornwallis's 6,000 men. Some 13,000 French seamen rode at anchor in Chesapeake Bay. All together, the swollen population of the Yorktown environs made it momentarily a rival of Philadelphia, the largest New World city north of Mexico.

Custom called for all trenches to be dug and all cannon and mortars in place before the bombardment could begin. The allies launched their labor. "General Washington ... struck a few blows with a pickaxe," wrote Sgt. Joseph Martin, "...a mere ceremony, that it might be said: 'General Washington ... first broke ground....'"

On a clear, bright October 9, Washington ceremoniously touched a match to a cannon and fired the first American gun. One witness claimed Washington's cannonball actually crashed through a house "where many of the officers were at dinner ... discomposing the dishes, and either killed or wounded the one at the head of the table."

The allied bombardment commenced its "aweful music," in the words of one officer. Cornwallis's earthworks began to crumble.

"We have lost about seventy of our men," Cornwallis wrote Clinton one noon—and later added a grimmer comment: "P.S. 5 P.M. Since my letter was written . . . we have lost thirty men."

On the dark, rainy night of October 14, the French stormed one British redoubt near the river, and the Americans—under young Lt. Col. Alexander Hamilton—attacked another. Both redoubts fell.

"My situation here becomes very critical," Cornwallis wrote. He prepared one last desperate attempt: to cross the river—as Washington had done at Long Island—to Gloucester and escape to the north. But on the midnight that he tried this maneuver, a wild storm blew in and scattered his small boats. Cornwallis was doomed and knew it. He called for an officer, a white flag, and a drummer to rap out the call for parley.

About ten on the morning of October 17, Lt. Ebenezer Denny noted in his journal that he "had the pleasure of seeing the drummer mount the enemy's parapet and beat a parley. . . . I never heard a drum equal to it—the most delightful music to us all."

No one remembers the name of the lonely, frightened drummer boy who exposed himself to the duel of cannon. Yet the message of his drum drowned out all the noise of war.

Tina asked our guide to help us find this drummer's parapet. "Rob says that William Diamond started the war with his drum at Lexington," she explained. "So I guess this British drummer ended the war." But no one today can be certain just where he stood.

At least the Moore House is easy to find; it is the handsome farm home where the peace commissioners worked out the terms of British surrender. The youngsters sat in its sun-flooded parlor while I read them the terms signed here: Cornwallis's men would march out "with . . . Colours cased and Drums beating a British or German march."

"Sure!" said Kel. "Those Charleston veterans were getting even for their surrender."

They were, too. By military custom, brave defenders were permitted the honors of war: They could march out proudly, with colors flying. And they returned this courtesy by playing the victors' own music.

But now King George's vanquished men marched out between rows of Americans and French as required—to a British air. With a touch of irony, they selected "The World Turned Upside Down." Lord Cornwallis did not attend; he pleaded illness and sent his sword by his brigadier, Gen. Charles O'Hara, who tendered it into the hands of Charleston's defender, Benjamin Lincoln.

The formal, cow-pasture surrender ultimately meant what Lafayette said of it in a letter: "The play, sir, is over."

But not at once.

Citizens cheer Washington as he leads a victory procession into New York City on November 25, 1783; the

1782-83:
"The Storm Being Past"

LITHOGRAPH BY E. P. & L. RESTEIN, LIBRARY OF CONGRESS

British had evacuated their last major stronghold in the new republic after a seven-year occupation.

AT YORKTOWN'S SURRENDER FIELD, Josh perched himself on a split-rail fence, got a faraway look, and composed a poem. He titled it "Yorktown" and ended it this way:

> *The enemy, half deaf*
> *By boom of the cannon,*
> *Saw the boy standing there*
> *And stopped.*
> *The noise died down—*
> *And the sword was given.*

But Josh still had a question: "Did the war really end *right here?*"

I looked around the field; with six Angus cattle grazing, it certainly looked like a birthplace of peace.

"Yorktown was our last real battle with the British," I said. "There were some skirmishes, of course, and the British kept on fighting the French and Spanish for a while. Peace came slowly, and it took a lot of talking."

Gossips in London said that when Lord North learned about Yorktown, the Prime Minister knew the real meaning at once: Again and again, he wildly exclaimed, "O God! It is all over!"

But King George reacted with stubborn optimism: "when Men are a little recovered of the shock...they will then find the necessity of carrying on the War...."

Nor would Washington assume the war was over. "My greatest fear," he wrote, "is that Congress...may think our work too nearly closed...." He prepared to meet the British offensive of 1782. It never came.

Instead, a new British ministry began negotiating peace in April, 1782, with Benjamin Franklin in Paris—and later also with John Jay, John Adams, and Henry Laurens.

But negotiations between Britain and France bogged down over Gibraltar. Spain still hoped to take it back from England.

The war goes on: Beyond the rugged slopes of Îles des Saintes near Guadeloupe in the West Indies, guns thundered in 1782 when British Admiral Rodney crippled the French fleet. Taking advantage of a shift in the wind, he plunged through the line of enemy warships, blasting and disorganizing them. H.M.S. Barfleur *(below, center) cannonades the huge French flagship* Ville de Paris, *commanded by Admiral Count de Grasse. Survivors continue the battle in open boats. The victory gave Britain supremacy in the West Indies.*

NATIONAL GEOGRAPHIC PHOTOGRAPHER WINFIELD PARKS; CONTEMPORARY ENGRAVING UNITED STATES NAVAL ACADEMY MUSEUM

Since Spain was France's ally—but not an ally of the U.S.A.—Franklin and his colleagues quietly talked with the British alone.

On April 12, 1782, His Majesty's navy fought two battles against the French on opposite sides of the planet. In the crystal Caribbean, Admiral Sir George Rodney overtook the Count de Grasse's fleet near the isle of Guadeloupe. Breaking the formal rules of sea warfare, Rodney and two of his captains sailed straight through the line of French ships, splintering De Grasse's fleet into four fragments and inflicting terrible damage. De Grasse struck the colors on his 110-gun flagship *Ville de Paris,* the world's mightiest war vessel and a veteran of Yorktown. Britain now ruled the waters of the West Indies.

On the same day off Ceylon, the admirals Hughes and Suffren contended for the waters

around India; but the engagement lacked a clearcut victor. The distant, imperial forces of Britain and France continued to spar while diplomats danced their own stylized minuets.

Talks continued through the hot summer. Franklin recalled an anecdote of ancient times that he now told the British. A small defeated state begged the Roman Senate for peace. How long would peace last, wondered the Romans. "That would be according to the conditions," Franklin quoted the ambassador; "if they were reasonable, the peace would be lasting; if not, it would be short."

The English-speaking diplomats decided on a reasonable and lasting peace. Without the help of allies, the British and Americans secretly devised and then signed a separate preliminary peace treaty in Paris on November 30, 1782. Great Britain recognized the

187

England's difficulties in America deepen, and bitter European rivalries—fueled by British victories in earlier wars—flare up in battles from Hudson Bay to the Indian Ocean. World-wide involvement, and fear of invasion at home, diverted British funds, troops, and ships, preventing concentration on the war in America.

GREENLAND
UNEXPLORED

UNEXPLORED

Hudson Bay

NORTH AMERICA

UNEXPLORED

CANADA

Newfoundland

LOUISIANA
(Spain)
UNEXPLORED

UNITED
STATES

Azores

Bermuda

MEXICO
(Spain)

EAST FLORIDA

ATLANTIC OCEAN

WEST INDIES

Cape Ve
Islar

Caribbean Sea

Îles des Saintes

(Spain)

PACIFIC OCEAN

BRAZIL
(Portugal)

SOUTH
AMERICA

UNEXPLORED

(Spain)

Falkland Islands

DETAIL OF PAINTING BY JOHN SINGLETON COPLEY, THE TATE GALLERY, LONDON

RARE BOOK DIVISION, LIBRARY OF CONGRESS

ENGRAVIN

Maj. Francis Peirson (top left) falls with a fatal wound as his British troops repulse French invaders on the Channel isle of Jersey. Left, the British governor at Senegal surrenders Fort St. Louis to French commander Duc de Lauzun during one of the attacks on British settlements in Africa. Right, in a futile grand assault Spanish ships explode off Gibraltar in 1782, ending a three-year siege of the British-held rock. Far right, French Admiral Suffren confers with Indian ruler Hyder Ali, whose army also fought Britain. The French and British fired the final shots of the war on Indian soil near Cuddalore.

SWEDEN

REAT
TAIN
Flamborough
Head
DENMARK

NETHERLANDS

EUROPE
PRUSSIA

FRANCE
AUSTRIAN EMPIRE

UGAL
SPAIN
Minorca

Gibraltar
SICILY

deira
ds

RUSSIA

SIBERIA
(Russia)

UNEXPLORED

A S I A

CHINA

JAPAN

BENGAL

INDIA

PACIFIC OCEAN

Malabar
Coast
Cuddalore

Ceylon

PHILIPPINES
(Spain)

GAL

AFRICA

UNEXPLORED

Sumatra

EAST INDIES
(Netherlands)

ANTIC OCEAN

MOZAMBIQUE
(Portugal)

INDIAN OCEAN

ANGOLA
(Portugal)

Madagascar

Mauritius

AUSTRALIA

UNEXPLORED

Cape Town
(Netherlands)

Great Britain and colonies

At war with British

Armed Neutrals

Uninvolved areas

• *Battles*

independence of the United States of America and the boundaries from the Atlantic to the Mississippi, from Canada to Florida.

It took Franklin only a few days to soothe the French—and to secure a new French loan.

Yet the world conflict that we call the American Revolutionary War was still not formally ended. In June of 1783 a British column was fighting a French garrison in the muggy forests along the Bay of Bengal. The two armies finally heard about the preliminary peace treaty while the warriors were engaged outside Cuddalore, India. The battle ceased on June 28, 1783, just eight years, two months, and nine days after Lexington—and in the land of that costly surplus of tea.

"Then was Cuddalore the last battle of the war?" asked Tina.

"Perhaps," I said, "if we don't count our frontier skirmishes with our Indians."

The final, formal treaty was signed at Paris on September 3, 1783. And at last Ben Franklin could say, "we are now Friends with England and with all Mankind."

So Yorktown, Cuddalore, and Paris can all make a valid claim to the war's end. But to me, a long log building near Newburgh, New York, calls up special, personal memories.

It was here at the New Windsor Cantonment that George Washington met the tests of uncertain peace, waiting for a treaty—or for renewed war. The unpaid soldiers were growing restless—and dangerous. Anonymous circulars were handed around ("Can you consent to be the only sufferers by the Revolution?"), and the air was thick with intrigue. Would this revolution, like others before and after, devour its own?

Washington called together the grumbling officers on March 15, 1783. They filled the hall called the Temple, which served for worship, dances, and conferences. He began to speak—carefully and from a written manuscript, referring to the proposal of "either deserting our Country in the extremest hour of her distress, or turning our Arms against it. . . ." Washington appealed simply and honestly for reason, restraint, patience, and duty —all the good and unexciting virtues.

And then Washington stumbled as he read. He squinted, paused, and out of his pocket he drew some new spectacles.

"Gentlemen, you must pardon me," he said in apology. "I have grown gray in your service and now find myself growing blind."

Most of his men had never seen the general

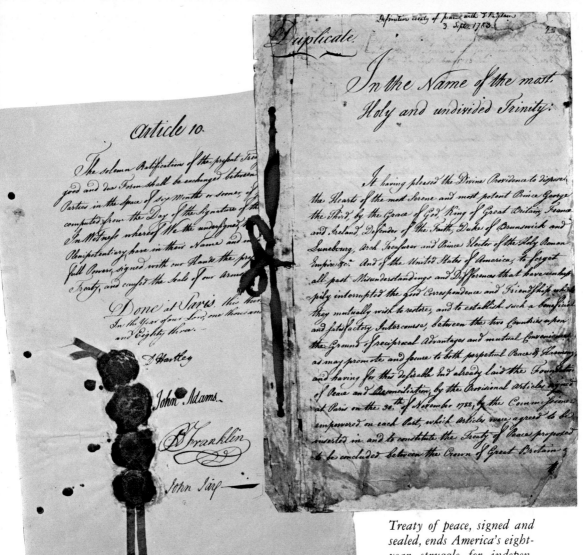

Treaty of peace, signed and sealed, ends America's eight-year struggle for independence, in Paris on September 3, 1783. The adroit American commissioners won the major terms that they had demanded for their new nation when they negotiated a preliminary treaty with the British nine months before. Delegates at the earlier signing sat for artist Benjamin West: (from left) John Jay, John Adams, Benjamin Franklin and Henry Laurens. William Temple Franklin, Benjamin's grandson (far right), served as secretary. A British delegate, self-conscious of his homely appearance, declined to pose and the canvas remained unfinished.

wear glasses. Yes, men said to themselves, eight hard years. They recalled the ruddy, full-blooded planter of 1775; now they saw the man of 51 who needed no powder for his hair. A big, good, fatherly man grown old. They wept, many of those warriors. And the Newburgh plot dissolved.

At the same Temple door just one month later, news of the armistice was "publickly proclaimed" and thanks offered "to almighty God for ... causing the rage of war to cease. ..." The date was April 19, "a day which compleats the eighth year of the war."

I read those words from Washington's general orders as I stood on the same spot, in the

Choked with emotion at taking leave of his comrades, George Washington throws his arms about faithful Henry Knox at Fraunces Tavern in New York on December 4, 1783. He embraced each officer; then, with tears misting his eyes, walked to a waiting barge to begin the long journey home.

doorway of the restored Temple; outdoors the green of springtime flooded full. What deep happiness those men must have felt in the first peaceful springtime of our nation!

The last British troops marched from New York on November 25, 1783, "equipped for show ... with their scarlet uniforms," a woman recalled; the patriots marched in, "ill-clad and weather beaten ... but then they were *our* troops ... and my eyes were full...."

At Fraunces Tavern a week later, George Washington said goodbye to his officers. He had no speech to read and he could hardly trust his voice for the few words he spoke: "With a heart full of love and gratitude, I now take leave of you. I most devoutly wish that your later days may be as prosperous and happy as your former ones have been glorious and honorable." The comrades lifted wine goblets, and Washington continued, "... I shall feel obliged if each of you will come and take me by the hand." Henry Knox was the first, his hand outstretched. Washington's blue eyes filled—and he threw his arms around the shoulders of his bulky friend. Each comrade followed weeping. And through it all, no one spoke a word.

Still not trusting himself to speak, the general crossed by barge to the New Jersey shore. As we followed his route by car and map, Josh remarked that "Washington must have relived the whole war on his way home." Retreating across New Jersey, passing through Trenton, crossing the Delaware in December, seeing Philadelphia almost on the anniversary of his Valley Forge arrival, then on past Germantown and Brandywine ...

Congress was meeting in Annapolis, and there, on December 23, General Washington returned his commission with a trembling hand. Early that afternoon, the civilian planter set out, hurrying to Mount Vernon. His goal was the simple hope of every returning soldier: to be home by Christmas.

As his knees gripped the trotting horse, George Washington must have pondered the future of his recent comrades and enemies.

"What did happen to all the veterans after the war?" Josh asked. We compiled a partial list. Poor George III, unwilling to accept American independence, had written out his abdication before the end of the war. He never sent it. In later life, he lost his mind. Lord North lost only his eyesight. And Ban Tarleton served stylishly in Parliament.

Dan Morgan matched his old enemy: He speculated in western lands, made money, and got elected to Congress, comparing his opponents to "Egg sucking Dogs."

Horatio Gates sold his Virginia plantation, freed his slaves, and lived on at his New York estate to a venerable age. Nathanael Greene moved south to lands that Georgia gave him, and there he died at the untimely age of 44; his friend Anthony Wayne was with him to say: "I have seen a great and good man die."

Henry Knox, of course, served as first Secretary of War for President Washington. And as a businessman, Knox grew rich. Those gifted financiers Robert Morris and Haym Salomon died poor.

Philip Schuyler and Aaron Burr defeated each other, at different times, for the governorship of New York. And Alexander Hamilton, who became a Wall Street lawyer and a statesman, married Schuyler's daughter—and died after dueling with Aaron Burr.

"And the Baroness von Riedesel—don't forget her," my wife reminded. The von Riedesels returned to Europe with many fond memories—and a baby girl named Amerika.

Von Steuben became a naturalized American and lived in New York on a pension arranged by friends. Lafayette returned to France, and survived the revolution there.

And a residence called the White House became the home of John Adams and later his son, of Jefferson, Madison, Monroe, and that redhead with a British saber scar on his scalp, Andrew Jackson.

"And the drummer boy?" asked Rob. "Not *me*," he explained—"the real Yankee Doodle one." He meant William Diamond of Lexington, who served through the whole war and became a wheelwright in New Hampshire, where he lived to the age of 73.

Just as we ticked off the names of 18th-century friends, so George Washington, riding home to his Martha on Christmas Eve, must have thought about all those close to him. His stepson Jack Custis was dead from camp fever caught at Yorktown; Washington would rear Jack's children as his own.

Perhaps he thought of his friend Bryan

Fairfax, soon to take holy orders in the Episcopal church. Washington would remember him in his will: to leave him his own Bible.

Perhaps he also thought about the future—the crops he would plant at Mount Vernon, the fish and the hams he would smoke and cure, the animals he would raise. No doubt, too, he thought of his country.

"We . . . have yet to learn political Tactics," Washington had written Lafayette. ". . . I fear . . . that local, or state Politics will interfere too much with . . . wisdom. . . ."

In a similar vein, John Adams had said: ". . . America is a great, unwieldy Body. Its Progress must be slow. It is like a large Fleet sailing under Convoy. The fleetest Sailors must wait for the dullest and slowest."

The most serene view of the future was Franklin's. He had urged Washington to visit Europe. "You would on this Side the Sea. . . . know, and enjoy what Posterity will say of Washington. For a 1000 leagues have nearly the same Effect with 1000 Years. . . .

"I must soon quit the Scene, but you may live to see our Country flourish, as it will amazingly and rapidly after the war . . . Like a field of young Indian Corn, which . . . by a Thunder Gust of violent Wind, Hail, and Rain seemed to be threatened with absolute Destruction; yet the Storm being past, it recovers fresh Verdure, shoots up with double Vigour, and delights the Eye not of its Owner only but of every observing Traveller."

The thunder-gust was over now on Christmas Eve. George Washington crossed on the Potomac ferry and rode downstream to that noble bank with its colonnade and peaceful view. He had reached the place he loved above all others, the spot where our own trail had started.

"Is the story all gone now?" asked Robert, very grown up and going on five when we visited Mount Vernon on a wintry day.

"The Revolutionary War is all gone," said Tina. "But the story isn't. All of us Americans are part of the story."

Mount Vernon glows in the slanting rays of a winter sun. On Christmas eve of 1783, amid the excited greetings of his family and servants, Washington strode through the door of the graceful mansion eager to resume the peaceful life of a country squire and to enjoy the blessings of liberty he had helped his nation win.

NATIONAL GEOGRAPHIC PHOTOGRAPHER GEORGE F. MOBLEY

Almanac

In the silence following the last roll of war drums, George III and his ministers had a startling set of facts and figures to ponder. A roster of ships and soldiers alone could never tell them why they lost the war, for as one of their countrymen observed, conquering America was "like trying to conquer a map." The land Britain claimed stretched across more than 1,000 miles of wilderness, loosely connected by rugged roads from New England to Georgia, and lay 3,000 miles over an ocean whose fickle winds might take messages and supplies across in a month, or delay them four. But King George, looking at military statistics in December, 1775, saw all of them weighing heavily in his favor.

British Navy: about 270 warships, 16,000 men.
British Army: about 7,000 regulars in the 13 colonies. Stores of arms, ammunition, artillery. Cash for payrolls and matériel.
Population (loyal subjects): 8,000,-000 in the British Isles and (by the estimate of the king and his cabinet) all but a willful minority of colonists.

Rebel navy: eight small ships.
Rebel army: 6,000 Continentals, short-term citizen volunteers with their own arms (not counting militia). Captured British cannon. Two small gun factories. Gunpowder imported. Paper money based on faith.
Population: about 2,000,000 (and 500,000 slaves). Patriots: enough to start a war.

In 1778, the power figures shifted. Now 217 French and 141 Spanish warships opposed Britain's 337. American private ships licensed to prey (3,700 by war's end) had in 20 months captured 733 British cargo vessels. The willful minority in the colonies looked more willful than minor, as evidenced by the departure from British-controlled cities of 20,000 out of 25,000 New Yorkers, 12,500 of 16,000 Bostonians, and 18,000 of 40,000 Philadelphians.

The figures at the close of the war:

British	United States
Troops (including colonists) maintained in North America for 7 years: about 50,000. Loyalists in the U. S.: not more than a quarter of the population; peak number of Tories in the British army, 8,200. Total military expenditure: $712,000,000 cash (in Spanish milled dollars; roughly, $7,000,000,000 [U. S.] today). No reliable figures have ever been established for the losses of warships, hundreds of merchant ships, and thousands of men.	Total patriot forces of the Continental Army and militia during eight years: an estimated 250,000, most serving short-term local duty. Washington's effectives for battle: from 6,000 to 28,000. Expenditure: $550,000,000 in Congressional and state paper money, plus other notes; also $8,000,000 in French loans and subsidies, $1,000,000 from Spain, $3,500,000 from bankers in the Netherlands. Lost: about 9,000 known dead.

The Thirteen States in 1780

State	Estimated Population	State	Estimated Population
New Hampshire	87,800	Maryland	245,500
Massachusetts (including present Maine)	318,500	Virginia (including present West Virginia, Kentucky)	583,000
Rhode Island	53,000	North Carolina (including present Tennessee)	280,000
Connecticut	206,700	South Carolina	180,000
New York	210,500	Georgia	56,000
New Jersey	139,600		Total 2,733,300
Pennsylvania	327,300		(Republic of Vermont... 47,700)
Delaware	45,400		

REVOLUTIONARY WAR DRUM, GUILFORD COURTHOUSE NATIONAL PARK

Index

Illustrations page references appear in *italics.*

Additional References

For additional reading, you may wish to refer to the following books and to check the *National Geographic Cumulative Index* for related material:

Background: Bernhard Knollenberg, *Origin of the American Revolution: 1759-1766;* John C. Miller, *Origins of the American Revolution.*

General accounts: John R. Alden, *The American Revolution 1775-1783;* Miller, *Triumph of Freedom 1775-1783.*

Biographical studies: Alden, *General Gage in America* and *General Charles Lee;* George A. Billias, ed., *George Washington's Generals;* Catherine Drinker Bowen, *John Adams and the American Revolution;* Esther Forbes, *Paul Revere and the World He Lived In;* Douglas Southall Freeman, *George Washington,* 7 vols.; Louis Gottschalk, *Lafayette . . . ,* 4 vols.; Dumas Malone, *Thomas Jefferson . . . ,* 5 vols.; Samuel Eliot Morison, *John Paul Jones;* Carl Van Doren, *Benjamin Franklin;* Willard Wallace, *Traitorous Hero . . . Benedict Arnold;* William B. Willcox, *Portrait of a General: Sir Henry Clinton. . . .*

Military studies: Troyer S. Anderson, *The Command of the Howe Brothers . . . ;* Allen French, *Day of Concord and Lexington;* William M. James, *The British Navy in Adversity;* Lynn Montross, *Rag, Tag, and Bobtail;* Howard Swiggett, *War Out of Niagara;* Wallace, *Appeal to Arms;* Christopher Ward, *War of the Revolution,* 2 vols.

Political and social studies: Carl Becker, *The Declaration of Independence;* Carl Bridenbaugh, *Cities in Revolt;* Edmund C. Burnett, *The Continental Congress;* Montross, *The Reluctant Rebels;* L. B. Namier, *England in the Age of the American Revolution;* William Nelson, *The American Tory.*

Diplomacy: Samuel Flagg Bemis, *Diplomacy of the American Revolution;* Richard B. Morris, *The Peacemakers.*

Collections of contemporary material: Henry Steele Commager and Richard B. Morris, *The Spirit of 'Seventy-Six;* George E. Scheer and Hugh E. Rankin, *Rebels and Redcoats;* Kenneth Roberts, *March to Quebec.*

Composition by National Geographic's Phototypographic Division, Herman J.A.C. Arens, Director; John E. McConnell, Manager.
Printed and bound by Fawcett-Haynes Printing Corporation, Rockville, Md.
Color separations by Lanman Engraving Company, Alexandria, Va.; Beck Engraving Company, Philadelphia, Pa.; and Graphic Color Plate, Inc., Stamford, Conn.